Reactionary!

by **SGT. LLOYD W. PATE**

as told to **B. J. Cutler**

Harper & Brothers

Publishers — New York

A shorter version of this book was first
published in the *New York Herald Trib-
une* under the title SOLDIER ON THE HOOK

Reactionary!

One

JUST before I was born my father killed a man. Ever since then everybody has been down on him, the law and everybody else. Even his family and friends looked down on him. I knew this when I was growing up and I made up my mind to show them our family was better than they thought. That was one reason I joined the Army before I was sixteen and it took me to Korea and into the Chinese prison camps. It also brought me back.

I was born on January 11, 1934, in Columbia, South Carolina. My father was William Carson Pate and my mother's maiden name was Evelyn Crossland. Their people had lived in the South for a long time. My dad is a big man and he's always been a heavy drinker. He was a truck driver, the best damn truck

1

driver I ever saw. He can take a forty-foot semi-trailer truck and park it in a spot where the average driver can't put a Crosley.

The day his trouble started he walked into a place where this guy made a slurring remark about my mother. My dad slapped him across the face and they started to fight. The man was noted for his ability to use a knife and he started reaching in his pocket as if he was going for his knife. So my dad took a pint of whiskey and broke it on the side of the man's head. The bottle cut his skin and knocked him unconscious. In a few minutes he came to and my dad gave him a quarter to go to the doctor and get bandaged. It cost ten cents for a cab and fifteen cents for the doctor. You can tell by these prices it happened quite a while ago.

The man took the quarter and left, but he didn't go to the doctor. Two weeks later he was found dead near the railroad tracks. An autopsy showed that the blow he received from the whiskey bottle was the cause of his death. And so they picked my dad up and tried him on charges of manslaughter. He was found guilty and I believe he pulled twenty-three months before he got out. Ever since then the law is picking him up every time he turns around or something like that.

My parents separated and went back together

more times than I can remember. The main reason was my dad's drinking, I guess. They finally broke up for good and my mother remarried when I was in Korea. She is living a very respectable life and has a nice home in Jacksonville, Florida. As a kid I was with my mother very seldom and with my dad even less.

In the little time I was with my dad, he taught me some things I've always remembered. He always told me never to tell a lie, even if it hurts you. He said treat the other man the way I wanted to be treated. Never to fight dirty, even if the other man fights dirty.

Down in my part of the country you can swear at a man but it's not a good idea to call him a son of a bitch. A man might kill you for that and the jury can turn him loose. The main thing my dad taught me was if a man calls you a son of a bitch, just laugh at him because anybody can look at you and see that you're not a dog. But if he calls you a damned liar, then try to kill him because nobody can just look at you and know you're not a liar.

I damn sure am not ashamed of my dad. His only mistake was just to let whiskey run his life for him. He's always been a fair man and he's always been just and willing to help any man out. My dad is always speaking his mind; that's why he's always in

trouble. If he doesn't like you, he'll tell you. If he does like you, he'll die and go to hell for you.

Because my parents were separated, I lived all over the place, mostly with my grandmother, Mrs. Sarah Crossland, in Columbia, and with my aunts in Jacksonville. My grandmother is actually the one who reared me. She taught me wrong from right and helped me get what education I have. I look on her much more as a mother than I do my real mother.

When I went to church it was mostly with my grandmother. She's a very religious woman and it was her influence more than anything else that put religion in my mind. At one time I went to church almost every night and two or three times on Sunday. Mostly Baptist and Methodist churches. I believe every religion has its good points and its bad points and I just more or less drew something from all of them and let my conscience be my guide.

My life wasn't all school and church. I had fun playing ball with the neighborhood kids. Most of all I liked to go fishing with my uncle, W. V. Neber. He was assistant manager of the cab company in Jacksonville and he was a great sportsman. He didn't care who won, just as long as the game was fair. "If you lose, don't cry about it; if you win, don't brag about it," he used to tell me.

At the age of twelve I became a delivery boy for

a store. I worked after school and in the summer. Later on I was a helper on a truck. Then at thirteen I became a bartender in a roadhouse on Highway No. 1 in Dinsmore, just outside of Jacksonville. I was big for my age and looked a lot older. This place was a tourist court and a call house, too. If you had the money you could get a woman. They also sold bootleg whiskey. It was everything combined into one. You name it, if we didn't have it we could get it.

My job was just tending the bar and sometimes breaking up barroom brawls. In addition to everything else the roadhouse was a gambling joint under cover. The law was being paid off. Sometimes I had to deal in the house games. They were strictly honest, just illegal as hell. I lived at this place and worked after school, from around three o'clock in the afternoon usually until we closed at four in the morning. I had no set salary. Just what I needed. If I wanted any money, I would just take it out of the cash register, sign a receipt for it, and that's all there was to it. My grandmother was in South Carolina at the time and she didn't know where I was working.

While I was working at this place, I sometimes used to go out with some kids at night and we'd help ourselves to chickens from a farm down the road. The owner and some of his helpers took out after us a few times but they never caught us. Sometimes

we even sent him invitations. "We got a bunch of fried chicken over to the place," we'd say. "Come over and help us eat them." He always complimented us on the chickens. He said they were the best damn chickens he ever ate.

There was one old buzzard who had a large watermelon patch near where we lived. One night we were planning on grabbing a few watermelons and we went down the country road that ran along his patch. We saw him sitting in his field and asked him what he was doing. He said he was waiting on some damn watermelon thieves to try to steal some of his watermelons. "Why, hell," we told him, "we'll help you. We'll sit with you."

"Why, fine," he said. "Come on over."

So we went into the field and sat in a long single line that stretched back to the road. We all sat on watermelons. One by one we snapped the vines from the watermelons we were sitting on and rolled the melons to the guys behind us. After a while when we figured all the watermelons would be out in the road, we just said, "Well, we don't think any watermelon thieves will be coming tonight and we'd better be getting back home." We walked back to the road, picked up our watermelons, and left.

Now I see what we did with the chickens and watermelons was wrong to a certain extent. I can't

say I'm sorry for it because I enjoyed every minute of it.

I stayed at the roadhouse for about eighteen months. Then I just got fed up with the whole damn works—it was so rotten and corrupt. I learned the facts of life there at an early age, about clip joints, sex, and how damn rotten people can be. I saw just how they wound up in the end and made up my mind to have a better life than that.

It wasn't all bad, though. Through my experience in the roadhouse I learned how to get along with people. I learned how to sit down and talk with a man and decide whether he could be trusted, if he was reliable. That probably saved my life later on in Korea.

I left that place about the time I finished the ninth grade in school. That was the last schooling I got. I went to work as a stockroom man in a grocery store, but I wasn't satisfied. I wanted to travel and see part of the world. Something told me there would be a war, and for some unknown reason, I don't know why, I wanted to be in it. So after a few months in the store I joined the Army.

Two

ABOUT a month before I was sixteen, I joined the regular Army in Jacksonville for a five-year enlistment. I remember the date was December 9, 1949. I just lied a little and told them I was seventeen. The Army was hunting for regulars at that time and didn't ask for a birth certificate.

I asked for the infantry because an uncle of mine, more like a brother to me, had been turned out of the infantry with a dishonorable discharge. I just wanted to make it up some way or another, to prove to some people back home that some of us could go into the Army and make a go of it.

My uncle had been with another man when a jeep was stolen. They parked the vehicle and the man went into some place. My uncle just sat in it. The M.P.'s came by and noticed the jeep. They picked

my uncle up and threw him in the stockade. And because he wouldn't rat on this other man, they just threw the book at him.

The Army sent me to Fort Jackson, South Carolina, for my basic training. I wasn't a goof-up and then, too, I wasn't an ideal soldier. I was just regular run of the mill. Basic wasn't tough. I wasn't used to taking orders, but I soon got accustomed to it and it didn't bother me. I liked the Army, I actually did. It was then I decided I might make a career out of it.

To me it looked a clean life. You met a lot of swell kids from all walks of life, from rich families and poor families, from all over the world. It was very interesting because you met people you never even knew existed before. I just like to analyze people and there was the chance. There was always a turnover of new people, new faces.

By seeing what went on in basic I learned some things about getting along in the Army. They were mostly things not to do—don't be dirty, don't do any stealing, and don't shoot off your mouth and brag too much.

Take this kid who wouldn't take a bath. You could smell him from one end of the barracks to the other. We asked him to take a bath and he told us to mind our own business. We told him if he didn't take a bath, we'd give him one. He still wouldn't bathe.

Then about four of us crawled on him and took him to the shower. We turned on the hot water, took G.I. brushes and strong soap, and damn near skinned the poor guy. After that he didn't want another bath like we gave him. He took a bath at least once a day. We got all the dirt off him and he saw to it that no more got on him.

Then a lot of money came up missing in our barracks. Also watches, rings, and stuff like that. One day a group of us all chipped in some money and gave it to this one kid. It amounted to a little over $200 and we figured it was the bait to catch the thief. The kid put it in his billfold and started flashing it around. Then the lights went out, taps played, and he threw the billfold on his locker. We all went to bed. A few hours later one guy got up. He went to this kid's bunk, took the money out of the billfold, and started back to his bunk. About five of us grabbed him. We took the money off him, took him over to the stairs, and threw him down the damn stairs. We went down and grabbed him by the ankles, dragged him up the stairs, and threw him down again. Then we told the C.Q. we caught the man stealing money and he tried to escape and fell down the stairs. The last I heard he was up for court-martial for theft when he got out of the hospital.

And there was this guy who was always boasting

how good he was, how much he could drink, how he could hold it. He was always saying how observant he was. One day he came in pretty high and fell asleep. You might say he passed out. So we took four foot lockers and put his bunk on top of them. That put his bunk about four feet up off the floor. Then we hollered, "Fall out!" He was so observant he damn near broke the floor when he fell out. He quit bragging.

I learned in basic that a group that sticks together can damn near do what they want to. That's about it.

From Jackson I was sent to Camp Stoneman, near Pittsburg, California, for shipment overseas. There wasn't much to do at Stoneman but wait. I waited for about a month and then early in June I was shipped out on a military transport. It took fifteen days to get to Yokohama, Japan. I was assigned to the 519th M.P. Battalion. We patrolled the town and guarded 8th Army headquarters.

On the 25th of June I was in an illegal house drinking. As I came out, my C.O. came up and called me over. He told me that North Korea had invaded South Korea and that we were alerted for immediate shipment. It's not every day that a war starts so I finished my drinking before I reported back sometime that night or the next morning.

In the morning I put in my application to go to

Korea with the infantry. They tore it up and told me the plan was to keep the M.P.'s together and send them over as a unit. After that I put in several more applications but they were all turned down. I heard a rumor that if you goofed up, they would send you to Korea as punishment. I started goofing up—not passing the inspections, drinking too much, just making a general nuisance of myself. It worked, even though the rumor may not have been true.

The Army loaded men like me and regular infantry replacements on a Japanese boat and on August 29 we landed at Pusan. We didn't hold much of Korea then, and looking at it you couldn't see why anyone would want to.

I had been in Japan, so Korea didn't smell too bad, even though they use human waste for fertilizer. Most of the buildings were made of mud and sticks and had thatched roofs. It was a very dirty country and the climate was rough. In the summertime it will melt the ears off a brass monkey. In the wintertime it will freeze them off. So a poor brass monkey doesn't stand much of a chance. In the summer the older women go around naked from the waist up, but they weren't much to look at.

From Pusan I went to a replacement depot, and from there I was shipped a few days by train to King Company, 19th Infantry Regiment, 24th Infantry

Division. I was put into the second squad of the fourth platoon as an ammo bearer for a 57 mm. recoilless rifle. My job was seeing that the weapon had ammo at all times, helping to take care of the weapon, and defending the weapon.

The day I got to the company was around September 1 and we pulled right into a convoy and went to our positions on the Naktong River. It didn't take long for our first casualty. We were standing around shooting the bull and trying to find out what the score was from the men who had been in action. My squad leader was holding a grenade in his hand and telling us how to use it. This Mexican kid was leaning the muzzle of his rifle on his foot. He was cleaning it with a toothbrush. We heard an explosion and thought something had happened to the grenade. The squad leader threw it away and hollered "Grenade!" It scared hell out of us and we hit the dirt. The Mexican kid started moaning. He had sent a round right through his foot. The way he screamed and hollered did something to me. That first casualty threw a scare into me that's still in me. It's just a fear of getting shot.

Three

THEY didn't waste any time sending us to the front lines. We relieved a unit that was under attack by the North Koreans. These Gooks attacked all that day, that night, the next day, and the next night. My squad was on the rear of a hill, guarding against the enemy getting in behind us.

On the second night we were called around to the front because the North Koreans were making their final assault on the hill. They opened up with a fresh volley of fire and we all dived for holes. I fell right on top of a man and I said, "I hope you don't mind company dropping in all of a sudden." He didn't say anything. I spoke again and he still didn't answer. So I reached down to feel him and he didn't have a head. I picked him up and threw him out of the hole.

During the day a lot of Gooks had been killed. The sun had shone on their bodies and caused gas to come up inside of them. The cool night air caused that gas to want to come out and it was making a rustling noise. All that night I kept hearing this noise. I'd holler, "Halt! Who goes there?" And I was scared speechless, you might say. The next morning it got light and I could see what the noise was. I busted out laughing at my stupidity.

At daybreak the Gooks made their big push. We held as long as we could and then the old man gave orders to move out. My squad leader got scared or something and left the 57 mm. rifle. I ran back, got it, and tumbled down the hill. It was the only 57 brought down the hill. We moved into a group of trees several hundred yards back from the hill and then we counterattacked. There was one Gook machine gun raising holy hell with our men. It was literally slaughtering them. My squad was told to get rid of the machine gun.

We managed to maneuver fairly close to the machine gun nest without losing a man. About the time we were ready to lower the boom on it, a damn potato-masher grenade came over and landed right in the middle of us. It got three of the men in the squad, wounded them pretty damn bad. I don't know

what happened to the other men in the squad. I was alone there with the weapon and all the ammo. A kid from another squad came by and I asked him to help me. We studied the position and saw the only way I could fire at the machine gun was to stand up straight, take aim, and fire. We figured I would be exposed two or three seconds.

I told this kid to make sure that nobody stood behind me. The back blast of a 57 is capable of killing a man up to seventy-five feet behind it. A South Korean came up and joined us. I motioned for him to stand out of the way and stood up with the 57. Just as I was ready to fire, he moved in behind the weapon. I ducked and we told him it would kill him if he stayed where he was. He nodded and got out of the way. As I got ready to fire again, he moved back behind me. Four times I warned him. Each time I had to expose myself to the Gooks and our men were still getting hit by the machine gun. Finally I jumped up for the last time. He moved in behind the weapon and I fired. It got the machine gun and just disintegrated the poor South Korean, but knocking out the gun was more important than one life.

We moved to another hill and tied in with Love Company. When it got light the Gooks attacked

again. They beat us down to a bunch of rocks where we held. Then Love Company went down to the base of the hill. Most of our men went with them. There were eleven of our men still on the hill. The Gooks started throwing mortars in on us. One landed close to a kid named Poole. A piece went under his arm, one hit his neck, and one went through his helmet into his head. It was sticking half in, half out. "My God, I'm hit," he said. He crawled over to a little rock, laid his head on that cool stone, and started calling for his mama. He died there.

Three of our jets came over and started raising hell with the North Koreans behind the hill. Then Corsairs came and relieved the jets. Then some English Spitfires and then some more jets. We didn't know at the time but the Gooks were regrouping behind the hill for a big attack. They didn't know we had only eleven men on the hill. The planes stopped them and our company came back up. We took the hill and started digging in.

At this time I met a kid named Ord who had come over from Japan with me. Since both our squads were wiped out, we went in together as foxhole buddies. Word came up for us to dig a hole right where we were. We were standing on a Korean grave so we took them at their word and dug down into it.

That night the Gooks started throwing artillery. I jumped in the hole and was asleep almost before I hit. Ord spread a poncho over me and walked into the woods to relieve himself. When the barrage let up, some medical corpsmen came up to take bodies off the hill. They must have seen my boots sticking out and thought I was a dead body. They put me on a stretcher and as they were taking me down the hill the bouncing woke me up. So I sat up and said, "What the hell's going on here?" The corpsman behind me let out a yell and dropped his end. The one in front looked at me, let out a yell, and ran off. They didn't like bodies sitting up and talking to them.

The next day a sergeant came up and told us to go around to the right into the valley. He wanted us to give a warning in case the enemy tried to come in from that direction. Shortly after we dug in the North Koreans put a machine gun on the hill in front of us. Every time Ord or I would stick our heads up, the machine gun would cut loose on us. At night one of the most beautiful moons you'd want to see came up and if we'd raise our heads, they could see us as plain as in the daytime. We were pinned down for three days in that position and the sergeant sent a missing-in-action telegram to my people. Finally a 75 got the machine gun and we made it out of there.

In the meantime all the lost ground had been re-taken. A few days later we pulled back into reserve with about 25 per cent of our original men. We stayed in a pear orchard three days. We shaved, took a bath, rested a bit, collected PX rations, and got a couple of beers per man. They put a few G.I. replacements and a lot of South Koreans in with us. The ROK didn't look like an army. They dressed in fatigues, in cotton padded outfits, in English clothes. Whatever took their fancy, they wore. Some were good men but a lot ran like rabbits under fire.

After the replacements arrived, we got word we were ready to push across the Naktong River. We got across on the 17th of September and found about five hundred bodies, including some Americans, buried up to their necks in the sand. They had been made to dig their own graves and then they had been stuck with bayonets and shot through the head. At first report General William F. Dean was among them, but luckily he wasn't and came back all right.

While we were investigating the bodies, I saw Ord coming out of the woods with some boxes under his arm. I asked him what he had and he said he didn't know. "Throw me a bayonet and we'll open them up," he said. "Maybe it's something to eat." He started beating on the boxes, trying to pry the boards

off. He was always all thumbs and I got impatient as hell. I took the bayonet away from him and started in on a box. By this time quite a few guys gathered around. I got a board off and could see a big cake of yellowish-white stuff in there. We thought it might be cheese so I knocked a chunk off and smelled and tasted it. It didn't have any smell and had sort of a salty taste.

By this time a lieutenant started elbowing his way through the crowd. "What've you boys got there?" he asked.

"Damned if we know, sir," I told him. "We just found them in the woods."

He got a good look at the boxes and jumped right up in the damn air. When his feet hit the ground he was running. "You goddamned fools," he hollered, "you got antitank mines there." I never saw a group of men disperse so fast as that crowd did.

We hit some resistance on the other side of the Naktong. In a few days it was all cleared up and we started pushing north. Nothing much happened: a few skirmishes here, resistance there, light here, heavy there. Pretty soon we found ourselves at the 38th Parallel. We stayed there for a few days. Then we got orders that we were going ahead, going up into North Korea. We were looking forward to

getting revenge for what they had done to our prisoners.

Sometime around the 1st of October we hit resistance. It was not too heavy, but not too damn light either. We had some pretty good fights there several times. I was first gunner for the 57 by now and was promoted to Pfc. We kept pushing and it looked like the North Koreans were through. The next thing we knew we were within spitting distance of the Yalu River.

Then it suddenly turned into a new war. The Chinese came in and hit the 1st Cavalry Division. We went over to help them out and fought for thirty-six hours with them. Our 1st Battalion got surrounded and we had to go help them out. On our way over we met five hundred Chinese and North Koreans face to face right in the middle of a damn road. We took a hill on one side of the road and they took two hills, one on each side. Between my company, a company out of the 21st Regiment, and the Air Force, we managed to get the best of them in just a few days.

It was in this fighting that our company commander got hit. Captain Johnson was one of the bravest men I've ever seen. When the going got rough, he didn't stand behind and push you. He got in front and led you. Our company felt it when he

got hit. There wasn't a man who wouldn't have followed him to hell with drawers soaked in gasoline just to see him kick the devil's ass, to put it mildly. He was standing in the middle of the road giving orders to the men when a mortar came in and got him in the shoulder.

My squad leader got hit in the foot at the same time. I became the squad leader as well as first gunner and I made corporal.

After that we started moving south again. We were withdrawing to the south, not retreating. A lot of people said it was a retreat, but I don't see how you can retreat when you have to fight your way south through enemy troops behind you. And that's what we did. I believe it was on the 4th of December when we crossed the 38th back into South Korea. We felt let down by the folks back home because we had a lot of confidence in MacArthur and felt that they weren't giving him enough manpower, weapons, ammo, planes, and bombers.

We moved into an assembly area below the 38th and stayed for four days. While we were there I had a premonition that if we went up on the line again, I wouldn't be coming back. I don't know what it was; something just told me. It had never bothered me before. Like every G.I., I had a good-luck charm.

Mine was a doll, about four inches high, with long blond hair and an evening gown with a red sash. I always kept her in my shirt pocket in Korea, but when I had that premonition, I decided she would be safer left behind with my personal gear. I just didn't want the Chinese to get her.

I told the men in my squad about my feeling, but when we went up to the line on December 8 nothing happened. The Chinks were on one side of the border and we were on the other. The reason we were there was to find out if they were going to cross the 38th or not. We also gave our men time to regroup and set up fortifications to the south along the Han River. Nothing happened until the 30th when Item Company relieved us and we were pulled back about two miles below our positions. We drew PX rations, had a hot meal, and a good night's sleep. Then we changed into clean clothes and just laid around all day of the 31st.

That afternoon they served steak for supper because it was New Year's Eve. My stomach felt a little bit funny and I didn't go eat. It was two years, seven months, and twenty days before my next American meal.

Four

THE Chinks hit around six o'clock that night. They broke through Item Company and began to surround them. We were sent up on the line as reinforcements and told to hold at all costs. There was one hell of a fight. The Chinks were all around us. Our artillery was landing as close as ten yards in front of us, trying to keep them off us. It just seemed that the more damn Chinks we killed, the more kept coming. We'd kill one and two would take his place.

Around three o'clock in the morning we got orders to move out to the right flank and join the 1st Battalion of our regiment. When we got there we were all supposed to move out together. The Chinese had practically completed their encirclement. We managed to make it to the 1st Battalion and we were

ordered to set up a perimeter and hold until the battalion made its escape.

As the last vehicle of the 1st went out of sight the Chinese finished the encirclement. We were trapped and had one chance in a hundred of coming out. Finally our C.O. gave orders that it was every man for himself. He said to break up into small groups and try to fight your way out.

From then on it was just more or less of a madhouse. A group of six of us stuck together. A Lieutenant Nelson was the ranking man. We were going down a ravine when a mortar landed right between his legs. Almost all of us got wounded by that one mortar. Lieutenant Nelson was beyond any hope. A sergeant had his ankle shattered and a hole through his thigh. I got a few pieces of shrapnel in my leg.

A buddy of mine, Cletys Nordin, from Oklahoma, and I got off that hill and reached the road. There was a steady stream of men and horses going south on the road. We thought they were South Koreans and fell in with them. In those days I couldn't tell a South Korean from a Gook or a Chink. They all seemed to wear any uniform that they pleased. Later I found out better.

Soon this Korean-looking soldier came by with a

The first thing that came into my mind was my grandmother. How would she take it? My being missing in action, not knowing, no letters coming. Would the shock kill her?

The Chinks came over and made sure we didn't have any weapons on us. Then they lined us up in a single file and marched us toward the hills. We had a couple of wounded men in the group and also a medic. When we got over to the bottom of hill they permitted him to patch up our wounded. Then they took us halfway up a hill and sat us down in the snow.

The guards they put on us came over looking for stuff they could confiscate. They took my Lord Elgin watch, my Parker pen and pencil set, a ring I had bought in Japan, my cigarettes, and some chewing gum. They got watches and rings off practically everybody in the group.

We just sat there the rest of the day in the snow. It was about thirty degrees below zero, maybe a little colder. We sat there watching the artillery and the airplanes playing holy hell with the Chinks all day long. They were getting it on the road, out in the fields, in the ditches, everywhere. On the other slope of the hill was a larger group of G.I.'s from King and Love companies. Artillery killed most of them and

got some of the Chinks, too. We were pretty lucky. Only a few rounds came near us and we didn't have any casualties.

That night the Chinks put a whole line of us up against a cliff. They put machine guns and Browning automatic rifles down in position and threw rounds into the chambers. The officer in charge raised his arm and I tackled Cletys Nordin and told him to keep his head down because they were fixing to shoot us. That is when a runner came up with a piece of paper for the officer. He read it and they had a little conference and pretty soon they started us marching.

They moved us down to the bottom of a hill. From every hill and ravine around there they brought Americans prisoners out. They walked us all night, mostly in circles. I passed out my Life Savers and gum while we marched. In the early part of the morning, the guards started falling out. They couldn't take it any more. Just at daybreak they put us in a little ditch and we stayed there all day with no food and no water except snow which we put in our mouths and melted.

As it got dark they bunched us all together again and started us marching. This time we marched in a zig-zag toward the south. Nordin had been hit in the

legs by the mortar that got Lieutenant Nelson and he
had trouble walking. I helped him the best I could.
By this time the Life Savers and chewing gum had
run out. and we were hungry. Our pants were also
frozen from sitting all day in the snow.

On the morning of January 3 we stopped in an
open field and they sat us down again. That afternoon they brought us a big wooden crock with our
first P.W. food. It was millet, a yellow grain a little
bit larger than pieces of sand. They had cooked it
but it was frozen by the time we got it. I took one
mouthful and spit it out. When I bit down into it, I
almost broke my teeth. Some guy said there were
rocks in it. I think it was diamonds because rocks
aren't that hard.

We were craving water and some sleep. None of
us had got any sleep since we were captured. During
the day we were afraid to go to sleep for fear we'd
freeze to death before we woke up. So we fought it
as hard as we could. At night we were walking. We
must have looked like a bunch of walking dead.

That night we started marching again. By this
time we were so worn out we could sleep as we
walked. They had one guard for each man. I had a
little Chink guard on me. He came up to my chest,
but he had a Thompson submachine gun. That was

enough to make him the biggest man I'd ever seen. He could speak a little Japanese and so could I. He gave me my first hope since I was captured.

The little guard said he had been a soldier under Chiang Kai-shek. He said he thought Chiang was a Number One man. He'd been captured by the Communists and forced into the Chinese Liberation Army. Then he'd been forced to come to Korea or else be shot. He wanted to go to Formosa and rejoin Chiang and he said he'd help me to escape if I'd promise him the Americans wouldn't shoot him and we'd send him to Formosa. I told him he wouldn't be shot and probably would be rewarded if he'd help me and some of the men escape.

This satisfied the guard and he told me we were following the lines south. He said the Chinese big wheels expected to push the Americans right off the peninsula and then they were going to turn us loose. But he thought the Americans would start holding and that the Chinks would hold us in an assembly area and wait for orders. He said at this time we would escape. It was all set as far as we were concerned. All we were waiting for was the lines to stop so we could bug out.

By this time we were carrying the Chinks' food and their ammo. A lot of the guys were even carry-

ing the guards' weapons. But we were all too damn tired to run, fight, or give a damn what happened next. I had nicknamed my guard Slim and I was carrying all his equipment. During the night of the 3rd, I slept through most of the march. A few times there'd be a bend in the road and I kept on walking straight. I'd wake up in the middle of a rice paddy with my little guard pulling on my sleeve.

The next morning they put about twelve of us in a corn crib. Our clothes dried out because we didn't have to sit on the ground. They brought us rice, about two tablespoons each. It was the best rice I'd ever eaten. It had some diamonds in it but it was still good.

We moved out that night and we still hadn't had any water. My thirst finally got the best of me. We passed a stream. It was frozen over but water was running underneath the ice. I fell out and started beating the ice with my fists until I broke a hole in it. This was against orders and Slim was begging, cursing and crying to make me get up. If he'd have shot me, he'd have shot me happy because I was getting my fill of water.

The end of the column went by and I was still drinking. They had guards at the end to bring up men who fell back or to get rid of them. One of them

starting kicking me in the ribs. He saw that wasn't doing any good and stuck me in the behind with his bayonet. I couldn't sit for two days. I got my cap full of water and double-timed back into my place in the column. I handed Nordin the cap. He drank some of it and gave the rest to another guy.

We wound up the next morning in a Korean village where a lot of us were put into a mud house. We stayed about a week and got food twice a day. It consisted of soybeans and rice. The guards who had brought us were relieved and I saw Slim march off. He took my hope of escape with him.

While we were in that village January 11 came and went. It was my seventeenth birthday and I was starting to think whether I'd live to see another one.

Five

AFTER the first shock of our capture wore off, the G.I.'s with me on those Korean mountain roads began to act like soldiers this country could be proud of. Some of us were sick and wounded. We were all half starved and unarmed, but we began to fight the Chinese. It was their stupid cruelty that made us want to fight.

The Chinks didn't like to march on those freezing nights any more than we did. But they were afraid of Americans airplanes and wouldn't go near the roads when it was light. To make themselves feel better they would kick us around and bayonet us. They didn't run us through, but just broke the skin and made us uncomfortable.

Their idea probably was to scare the G.I. and make

him an ideal prisoner. It didn't work because our morale was high at the time and it just made us mad. We started looking for ways to get even and it was surprising how much a prisoner could do to an armed guard.

Those Korean roads were mostly just paths through the mountains. A lot of them had cliffs going up one side and sheer drops on the other. These turned out to be our weapons. The Chinks didn't want any escapes and they always kept us on the side of the road against the cliffs. The guards walked on the outside of the roads.

When it was real dark we'd walk up close to a guard and just give him the hip or the shoulder real hard. He'd let out a yell and go over the cliff. It never caused any suspicion. As far as everybody was concerned, he'd just been sleeping on his feet and fell over a cliff.

I couldn't do much to the guards. For the first few days the little guard Slim was my ticket back home and I couldn't let him go over a cliff. After he left I got two or three of them. There was one kid in our column who got about twenty of them. The officers and the other guards never knew what was going on until they were going over themselves. We figured the more Chinks we got rid of there, the less there

would be on the line. A few of our G.I.'s were lost that way when they were sleeping and walked off a cliff.

Since the Chinese had us on a starvation diet we couldn't see why they should eat. Some of the men still had razor blades and knives left because the guards never searched them carefully, except for watches to steal. The Chinks carried their food in long narrow pieces of cloth that had been sewed like a sock. The men would slice the socks so the grain would spill out while the guards walked at night.

A lot of times we would pass oxcarts heading toward the front lines. They were loaded with 220-pound sacks of grain for the soldiers at the front. The boys with knives would stumble against the oxcarts and slash the bags. By the time the carts had gone a few miles most of the grain had run out.

Every night the road was jammed with Chinese soldiers heading toward the front. The first thing I noticed about them was their smell, mostly made up of garlic. They had cotton padded uniforms and tennis shoes. Some didn't even have caps and gloves in that weather. A lot of them didn't have weapons. Those that did had old Japanese rifles and a lot of American weapons. Their pack was nothing but a rolled-up comforter tied across their backs.

We didn't worry too much about the Chinese going south. I figured that the G.I.'s down on the front were still a hell of a lot better off than we were. And also we knew that by this time Uncle Mac had brought in enough men and weapons to kill them as fast as Mao Tse-tung send them. In a way we were glad to see them going south because most of them wouldn't be coming back. We used to holler at them that they'd better enjoy the trip because it was a one-way ticket.

Almost every night we saw air activity someplace along the road. The Americans could have dropped a five-hundred-pound bomb any place along the road and it would have been paid for in Chink lives. That's how congested it was. They were deathly afraid of our air power and we weren't supposed to smoke or make a light at night. The guys were always walking around with a cigarette or lighting one. The idea was to make enough light. Then a Chink would come along and kick you in the behind for it.

One night we were crossing a long and pretty high concrete bridge that had been bombed before and repaired with planks. A B-26 came over. He couldn't have timed it any better because just as the last men in our group got off the bridge, he dropped his load. I think there were several thousand Chinese

killed by that one plane when the bridge collapsed. We didn't lose a prisoner to air action although we had some close calls.

Of the Chinks coming south, the ones we hated the most were the mule-cart drivers. Those bastards had whips and a lot of men including me carried welts across the face where they used them on us. The foot soldiers didn't bother us because we were bigger and heavier than they were. We used to run into them with our shoulders to see them go sprawling in the snow and mud. It's a wonder a lot of them weren't trampled to death because the Chinks behind would walk right on over them. By the time they got up we'd be out of reach and our guards wouldn't let them at us anyway. A lot of times, though, the Chinese passing by would let you have it in the stomach when you weren't expecting it.

We stopped in a village one day and the Chinks came around to ask who had drivers' licenses. They said they wanted men who could drive trucks to take the American wounded off the front lines. Some of the men said they could drive trucks and the Chinks took about a half a dozen of them out. They caught up with us a few weeks later and we found out what had happened.

The Chinese had captured quite a few of our trucks.

They wanted these men to haul ammunition and food to the Communist forces on the front. The men flatly refused until the Chinese brought in guards and told them they'd be shot if they didn't drive the trucks.

They put a Chinese guard in each truck along with one of our drivers. The guards were afraid of our bombers and they were always in a hurry. At first our men would slow down behind a column of troops, but the guards would motion them to hurry up. So they'd just throw the trucks into second gear and plow through the column. The Chinese would think nothing of it if one of our drivers killed a dozen of their soldiers. But if they so much as brushed one of the Chinese pack mules, the guards would go crazy. They almost shot drivers for this several times.

Our drivers wrecked the trucks by whipping them off the roads when they could. The Chinks didn't know anything mechanical about trucks and they'd make the G.I.'s get underneath to fix them. So they'd just tear the trucks up some more and the Chinese never knew the difference.

A few times the truck guards would fall asleep at night and they didn't wake up again. The drivers would wait until they got to the top of a cliff. Then they'd jump out and let the trucks go over, guards and all. When the Chinese would ask our man what

happened, he'd just say the brakes gave out. Then they'd get him another truck and another guard.

Whenever we'd come into a village the South Koreans were very unfriendly. The kids and grown-ups would run out and sick their dogs on us. They would spit on us, kick us, curse us, hurt us. Sometimes they'd even try to shoot us. They fired at one kid and nicked his shoulder. I didn't think that after we had fought for South Korea they would turn on us, but that's what they did. I believe they really hated us.

This happened the whole time we were in South Korea. They were always pointing and laughing and making fun of us. When we were put in Korean houses for the day, they wouldn't give us any water, not because they didn't have it but because they didn't want to. One Korean came up while we were marching, cleared his throat, and spit in the side of my face. I grabbed him and spit right in his damned face and hit him with everything I had behind my fist. He hit on the ground and didn't move. I hope I broke his neck but I think I just knocked him out.

On the 24th of January we were in this big village about forty miles southwest of Seoul. The Chinese came around and asked about the wounded men, who was sick, who had heart trouble, and so forth. They told us we were fixing to go on a long march north

to a P.W. camp on the Yalu River where they had nice warm buildings, fresh vegetables, mountains of beef and pork, candy, cigarettes and soap—a place where we would be comfortable and very happy.

They said they only wanted the strongest men to try and make the march. The sick and wounded were to remain in the village and then be taken to the front lines and released. Everybody faked some sort of sickness but the Chinese saw through that. By this time we had about four hundred men. Out of the whole group only thirty-five to forty were picked to stay back. We found out later that they had been turned loose, all of them.

The next night we started our long march north. It was nothing but a hellish nightmare from then on. And when we got to their wonderful camp it got even worse than a nightmare.

Six

WHEN we started walking north, the Chinese said it was about a five-hundred-mile march. They said they were fixing the rail line and we would catch a train as soon as we hit a point where the railroad had not been bombed out. This turned out to be a typical Chinese promise. We didn't see a train for more than two years.

We marched at night and slept in Korean houses during the day. By this time our clothes were loaded with body lice. They hadn't let us wash since we were captured, not even our hands. All the men had boots, though, even the ones who had been barefooted. The men who had two pairs fixed them up. This was lucky because it was our feet that gave us the most trouble.

Walking all night our feet would sweat. Then when we got to the village where we were going to bed down, we had to stand in the snow anywhere up to two and a half hours before they finally found a place for us to sleep. Our feet would freeze and that was the most miserable part of the whole damn march.

Then we'd go into our room and try to take off our shoes—if there was enough room to sit down. Most of the time our socks were frozen to our shoes and our feet frozen to our socks. When we'd pull the socks off the soles of our feet would come off with them. Our feet looked like bloody pieces of meat, beef or pork that had just been butchered. But we had to get our socks off to massage our feet. If we didn't they'd freeze.

A lot of times we'd pull into a village where the Chinese would cram a hundred men in a small room. Half the men would squat down and sleep while the rest stood up. Later we'd change around. We didn't get to massage our feet in places like that and I lost my toenails and the skin on the bottom of my feet. About this time the pieces of shrapnel I had got in my leg the day I was captured began to bother me. I got a piece of tin and honed it down on a rock and cut them out.

No man ever dropped out of our column because of his feet. We carried them when they couldn't walk. We couldn't leave a man as long as he was living. It never entered our minds whether the Chinks would shoot him or not. It just was that he was an American and we weren't going to leave him.

The morale of the men was still high. It was due to the fact that we had left the sick men behind and they knew where we were going. We knew that the Americans were holding and we felt deep down inside that once the American forces started pushing north, nothing in hell could stop them. And we felt that if there was any way for them to liberate us, or help us, or get food to us, they would do it.

When we slept in these Korean villages, the Koreans would be in one part of the house and the G.I.'s in the other part. It would be left up to the family what we ate. They could feed us anything they wanted, but they had to feed us twice while we were in the house. If they wanted to give us water it was okay. If they didn't it was also okay.

Some of the families fed us rice, but not very often. Most of the time we got millet, cracked corn, or sorghum. It amounted to about a cup of food a day. When you boil sorghum it's real slimy and it tastes like hell. Sometimes we would be given a sauce to go

with the food and help it get down, but it didn't help too damn much.

A few times we went into houses and the next day before we pulled out the people would run to the Chinese and tell them we had damaged the furniture, or the paper doors, or paper windows, or something. This was a lie. The Chinese would fall out the man they had accused and one of the English-speaking Chinese would curse him, kick him, and call him a warmonger and American imperialist. The Koreans would stand there and laugh.

One time a G.I. fell off an icy log while we were crossing a river and he got soaked. The weather at this time was a good twenty-five to thirty degrees below zero. In the next village a Lieutenant Tommy Trexler, from North Carolina, took a cotton comforter and put it around this man to keep him from freezing to death. That night when we started to move out the Koreans accused the lieutenant of trying to steal the comforter. The Chinese were going to shoot him but finally they changed their minds.

All these cases happened in South Korea. Not once did they happen in North Korea. I am not trying to take up for the North Koreans because to me a Gook's a Gook. But right is right and wrong is wrong and we were treated a hell of a lot better by our

enemies in North Korea than by our allies in South Korea. These are civilians I'm talking about. The North Korean soldier tortured prisoners and was a murdering bastard.

A couple of nights later we went back through our old positions on the 38th Parallel. As we crossed the hill we could look down into the valley and it looked like a new village had been built there. We were about half a mile off but there was a big moon and snow on the ground. We could see the outlines of what looked like low buildings. When we got closer it was one of the most ghastly sights any of us had ever seen.

What we took for buildings were the bodies of the Chinese and Americans killed in the battle of December 31 and January 1. They were stacked up like cordwood, the heads toward the middle of the pile and the feet sticking out. The stacks were about thirty feet long, twelve feet wide, and six or seven feet high. I don't know how many stacks there were; you couldn't start to count them.

Even by moonlight I could tell the difference between G.I.'s and the Chinks. The G.I.'s were barefooted. A lot were missing pants and shirts. Some were completely naked, but all of them were barefooted. The Chinese had taken their boots. The

Chinks still had their tennis shoes. They weren't any good so the Chinks didn't steal them. For every pair of naked feet I counted fifteen to twenty pairs of tennis shoes. It gave me a certain feeling of satisfaction to know that their casualties were so much higher than ours.

From this point on we were in North Korea. The morale of the men started sinking. The ordeal we were going through was beginning to show. Their faces were getting drawn. Their eyes had that hollow look to them. We were dirty, hungry, cold, praying for death to come. Every day it was the same damn thing, forty and fifty men being crowded in a room twelve by ten, being fed twice a day about half a cup of chow, getting water once every other day when we were lucky.

Shortly after we passed the 38th, we were lining up to pull out of this village when all of a sudden this Korean woman came right in the middle of us. She had her apron filled with boiled sweet potatoes and she started handing them out to us. The guards ran her off. By this time we were in two columns and she came back in between our lines. We just closed up so the guards couldn't get to her. When she finished giving out the potatoes, we made an opening away from the guards and they never did get her. I got a

potato and ate it skin and all. It was the most wonderful thing I had since I was captured. We found out later that this woman had given fried eggs and pork to the G.I.'s who stayed in her house. It was the first act of kindness I saw in a Korean.

Several times after this, when we would be moving through a village, the North Korean civilians would run out, get next to us, and start hitting us. Not hard, just enough to make it look good. At the same time they'd be stuffing food and tobacco in our pockets. They would spit at the Chinese and hold up their little fingers at them, which means you're number ten, or in English, you're no damn good. When the Chinks' backs were turned, they'd hold up their thumbs at us, which means you're number one, or you're the best.

At first I didn't know what to make of these Koreans. I finally got the opinion that they'd been under Communist rule before and they didn't like it, While the American forces were in North Korea, they'd had a little taste of freedom. They knew we hadn't come there to hurt them and they were more for us than their old government or the new one the Chinese were setting up.

About this time we entered the Pyongyang area and came to a P.W. camp which was later known as

the Bean Camp. It got its name from the only food
we got there—ground-up soybeans, corn, millet, and
maybe a little rice all compressed into a ball. It had
been a Japanese mining camp and the buildings were
mud on the inside with a thin sheet of cement on the
outside. Our planes had visited the camp and there
were shrapnel holes in the walls and roofs to let the
cold in.

There were prisoners in the Bean Camp when we
arrived and they said that quite a few men had already died there. It was there that we lost the first
men from our group. They were tired by now and
their wounds were beginning to get the best of them.
We left fifteen men there and heard later that most
of them had died. After about five days, we picked
up some English prisoners and marched to Pyongyang, where some more Americans joined us, and we
headed north again.

In one of the first villages we came to, they put us
in a house with one of the few happy Koreans I saw.
He fed us rice. Then he laughed, winked, and went
out again. He came back with a big bowl of one of
the best meats and sauces I have ever eaten. He let us
eat all the meat and rice we could. It was the first
meat I'd had that year and it was the last for quite
a while. After we'd finished, the Korean laughed and

told us it was dog meat in the sauce. We didn't care and wished we had more.

They changed guards on us at this point. The Chinese left and we got North Koreans. It threw a scare into us because we didn't know what in hell to expect, but everything turned out all right. They weren't any worse than the Chinks. On the road when the morale of the guys would get very low, Nordin and I would start singing. He was a wonderful tenor but I could never sing a note. We'd start laughing and making general fools out of ourselves. Then the men would start laughing and joking and they'd be okay for a while.

One night an Englishman had been singing in our hut when a guard came and opened the door. There was a bunch of Koreans outside and the guard motioned us to sing. We ignored him. Finally I got tired of hearing him hollering and raising hell and I stood up and told the guys to follow me in a song. I sang "God Bless America" and everybody joined in. An English-speaking guard heard the song and came over. When we got finished, he asked me for my name and I told him, but he never did anything about it.

A night or so later we came to this road that spiraled up around a mountain. Instead of following the road, the guards made us go straight up. It was like

trying to climb a ladder five hundred or six hundred feet high. About three-quarters of the way up I completely gave out. Two men, Sammy B. Lawing, from Seneca, South Carolina, and a kid named Stanford, from Oklahoma, grabbed me under the armpits and pushed and carried me up the hill. To these men I owe my life. If they hadn't helped me, I'd still be lying there.

Around the 3rd of March we started marching in the daytime. We knew we must have been pretty close to the camp or the North Koreans wouldn't have been so brave. Three days later we came to a frozen river. On the other side was Pyoktong, the end of our journey. It had been forty-one days since we started the march in South Korea.

We had one kid with us—all I remember him by is the name Tex—who hadn't eaten a bite in over two weeks. Nobody knew why. He hadn't drunk much water either. In the last village we stayed at, a Korean woman noticed at mealtime that Tex didn't eat anything. She went and made him a special noodle broth. He refused to eat it. As we were crossing the river that morning, Tex fell dead on the ice. A few feet further on a Spanish kid died.

After crossing the river, we climbed up the bank and walked about half a mile into Pyoktong. Our

B-29's had paid a social call a couple of months before and there wasn't too damn much left to see. As
we marched through town to the camp, I didn't
know I had yet to meet my worst enemies. My fellow
prisoners and hunger.

Seven

CAMP 5 was on the end of a peninsula in the Yalu River. We walked through Pyoktong to get to the camp, which was part of the town that had been fenced off. The camp wasn't what we had expected. It was nothing but a bunch of Korean buildings that had been bombed. The doors were missing, the windows were out, and it was just one big mess.

The men on the march with me took one look at the camp and right there half of them lost the will to live. It wasn't the camp that had the effect on them, it was the look of the prisoners they saw there. We had been on a death march for a month and a half, but they were in worse shape than we were.

As we went down the icy main road through the camp, we saw some American prisoners who had

been there for several months. They were much skinnier than any men I had ever seen. Their clothes and shoes were practically gone. Starvation was written all over their faces. I saw men who were well over six feet tall and couldn't have weighed a good hundred pounds.

The guards took us down the road. As we came to certain buildings they would drop off some men. They put twelve of us in a room, and as we filed past the Chink who was supervising it all pointed at me and said, "You'll be squad leader and monitor." The room was nine by twelve and completely bare. It just had four walls and a dirt floor. After a few minutes some of us walked outside to see what the hell we could find out.

I looked at the prisoners and couldn't believe that men could get like that and still be alive. A lot of them were barefooted. They were running to the latrine without any pants on. They had defecated in their pants and were too sick to wash them and didn't have another pair to put on. Some men couldn't wear any pants because their testicles were so swollen from beriberi that they couldn't pull their pants over them. I saw men with ankles puffed up as big as thighs. It looked like I could have touched them with a pin and they'd burst like a balloon.

Practically every man had dysentery. It was caused by the filth they had to live with and it just added to the filth. There was filth all over the place, in the rooms, on the ground, on the porches. The sick men couldn't make it to the latrine because of their weakened condition or the lack of control they had. It wasn't uncommon for a man to dirty himself or you, either, if you happened to be in the way.

The first day there, the Chinks called for a burial detail. I was on it with some of the men in my squad. We went into the death house and it was a sight I'll never forget. The bodies were stacked up and just thrown around the room. There were forty or fifty in there. Most of them were just young kids, seventeen, eighteen and nineteen. Some had clothes on and some didn't. They were nothing but skin and bones. But what got me most was the expression on their faces. Every one of them had his mouth open.

I used to read in books and magazines how a dead man had a look of satisfaction on his face, as if he was glad to die. But it wasn't so with these men. There was no look of satisfaction or smile of contentment. To look at them you'd think they were asking you to revenge them. They had suffered and died one of the most horrible deaths a man could have. That was a death by starvation. To know that they

died so damned unnecessarily put more hate in me than I thought a man could hold. If they'd been fed, they'd have been alive. It seemed to me that if the Chinese wanted to kill us, why the hell didn't they shoot us instead of letting us slowly starve to death.

We loaded the bodies on stretchers. They were made of rice sacks wrapped on two poles. Then we started them across the frozen Yalu River on their last ride. All told it was about a mile to Boot Hill. We had some shovels made of sticks and pieces of tin and we tried to dig a hole. The ground was frozen as hard as a rock and it was impossible to dig a grave with the tools we had. We scratched a shallow grave a few inches deep and laid the bodies in. We tried to straighten them out but it couldn't be done. They were already frozen and stiff. So we threw dirt and snow and loose rocks on them, said a little prayer, and left.

Late that spring the big thaw came and washed all the snow and dirt from the bodies buried in Boot Hill. We had to go over and rebury them. The Korean hogs had come in and started eating the bodies. It was one of the most sickening sights a man could see. Every place I looked there were bodies that had been chewed on by hogs. The ground was softer this

time and we buried the bodies and parts of bodies deeper than before.

After the first burial detail, we went back to the camp and tried to keep warm. Sometimes we'd all go into the room, hoping that our body heat would warm it up. If the sun was shining, we'd go outside and stand close to the building to keep out of the wind. But we had goose pimples all winter from the damn cold.

A couple of the best-fit men in each building did the cooking. The rest scrounged around for wood for them. We were supposed to be fed twice a day, but we'd get food once one day and three times the next. It was mostly cracked corn with some millet. Once in three days we'd get rice, which was a delicacy. Many a time we didn't get breakfast until four o'clock in the afternoon and supper until three in the morning.

The first morning a Chink threw open the door and asked in a half-baked English how many dead we had in there. It happened every morning from then on. Either a Chink or a North Korean would come. If you didn't have any dead in your room, he would stand there with the damn door open letting the cold air in and would cuss and raise hell. If you had one dead, he wasn't too bad. If you had two dead, he would even smile at you. If you had three or more

dead, he'd keep saying, "Ding Ho, Ding Ho." It means very good. And you'd just want to reach and grab him by the neck and watch his eyeballs pop out.

On my second day in camp I saw this guy come by. He was a fairly big guy, but no giant, and he looked to be in pretty damn good health. That's why I noticed him, that and his clothes. Except for the shoes, he was completely dressed in a Chinese cotton padded uniform. It was completely cruddy and so was he. We were all dirty but this man was three times dirtier. You could just tell his hair was strawberry blond under the dirt. It disgusted me to know that Americans were wearing Chinese uniforms.

A couple of days later, I was standing with a small group of men at the end of a building. We heard someone enter the room and say, "Move the hell over." A few seconds later the same voice said, in a very heavy Brooklyn brogue, "Goddamnit, when I tell you to move, that's what the hell I mean." At the same time we heard blows and moans coming from the room.

We all got around a window on the end of the building. The first thing I saw was the guy I had noticed a few days before in the Chinese cotton padded uniform. He was picking this man up off the floor in a pretty rough manner. He picked him up

bodily and carried him over to a corner where there was a steel peg sticking four to six inches out from the wall. Then he hung him on the peg.

I don't know whether he hung him by the belt, the pants, the shirt or even by the flesh. All I know is that the man was suspended off the floor. Then the man stepped back and laughed. He said, "There, God-damn you, that'll teach you when I say move, that's what I mean." And then he started messing around in the room.

I turned to this kid with me and asked him, "Who in the hell is that?"

"That son of a bitch is Gallagher," he said.

We held a quick conversation about this man. They said he was James C. Gallagher, a corporal from Brooklyn. I asked why they permitted such things to happen, and if this man was such a barbarian, why didn't someone kill him. They told me he was too strong for any of the men to try to take on and that the majority of the men were afraid of him because of his strength.

All this time I kept looking at the man hanging on the wall. I could see he was dead. In a few minutes Gallagher came back. He put his hand under the man's chin and snapped his head up. He held it there for a few minutes and looked at the man. Then he

let it fall. The head just lolled around when he dropped it.

Gallagher took the man down off the wall and carried him toward the door. I lost sight of him but I heard the door slide open and one of the men with me said, "The son of a bitch threw him out."

We went right around to the front of the building and there was the man laying crumpled up in the snow. I helped turn him over on his back and got my first real good look at him. Age was hard to determine in the camp because everybody looked at least forty, but from my experience with these men I would say he was eighteen or nineteen. He hardly had any beard. He was about my height—five-eleven —but he was nothing but a rack of bones. There were no signs of blows on his face. The blows had sounded like a fist or a boot in the stomach.

Five of us picked the man up and started to carry him to the death house. On the way over the others told me he wasn't the first man Gallagher had got. They said before I came to the camp he had got mad at two G.I.'s with dysentery who had been stinking up his room and threw them out in the snow to die. When we got to the death house I asked them if they knew this kid. They said no. I went through his pockets and searched his clothes for markings, for some

means to identify him. There weren't any. I never found out who he was.

That afternoon they called for another burial detail. We went to the death house to pick up the bodies as usual and this kid was still there. We loaded our stretcher up and I helped put him on last. Over at Boot Hill we went through the motions of digging a grave. I laid him in, threw the snow and dirt back on, and said a prayer. It was then that I made a vow to this boy and to his God and to myself that if God permitted me to live, to get back home, I would see that the man who had killed him would pay for it.

The Chinese pulled a big shake-up a few days later. They shipped me and my squad to Company 1 in another part of the camp. I never again saw any of the men who had been with me outside Gallagher's window that day. We were losing up to seventy-five men a day in that camp from starvation and dysentery and they may have died. It seems to me that if they had come back alive, they would have reported him.

In Company 1 we had the worst time in Camp 5. The men were cold, hungry, sick, lousy, and loaded with stomach worms. They were dying all over the place. We got the worms from the water and men were always pulling them out of their throats or throwing them up. Those worms just ate their stom-

achs out. There was one kid who died. When he died he was complaining about stomach pains. At least thirty minutes after he was dead, his stomach was still moving. Worms.

The lice were even worse than the damn worms. They killed quite a few men themselves, just drained every drop of blood in them. I saw one kid take off his shirt and throw it on the ground and it actually moved. A colored boy died and the doctors said lice had killed him. If you'd taken a pin and stuck it any-place on his shirt, you'd have stuck a louse. I honestly believe that if you'd left your shirt behind, it would have followed you.

We had an American Army doctor, a captain who had been captured in November, I believe. There are many men who came back from that camp owing him their lives. He had no medicine, no instruments, or anything else to work with. But he still worked wonders with the men. He pulled teeth with a pair of mechanic's pliers. The Chinese might give him a couple of aspirins, a half-dozen vitamin pills, and a couple of spoons of charcoal powder—for between two and three thousand men—but he still saved lives.

There was also a North Korean doctor. He used to come around and examine the sick men. Some he would admit to the sick compound, which we called

the death house because very few men ever came back from it. He would give you three little white pills and tell you to take them three hours apart. He'd promise that the next day you'd be Hokey Dokey. If you consider being dead Hokey Dokey, I guess they were Hokey Dokey. As far as I know they were poison because everybody he gave them to died shortly afterward. Sometimes he would give a man a shot right over the heart. That would finish him off.

The Chinese considered all this lenient treatment of P.W.'s. I know because that's how they said we were being treated. And they figured that now we were ready for their indoctrination program.

Eight

IT WAS late in April of 1951 that the Chinese in Camp 5 stopped trying to starve us to death. Instead they started trying to turn us into "good Communists." That was their name for collaborators, traitors, and guys who ratted on the other prisoners. I'm ashamed to have to admit that they succeeded in too many cases.

First they brought in meat and fish. The meat was green with mold and you could smell it a block away. It was liver, hearts, kidneys and tongue—all from hogs. The fish stunk to high heaven and was loaded with maggots. But it was better food than we had been getting and we were glad to eat it.

Even before this the Chinese instructors had been giving us short lectures about how we had been used

as the running dogs of the American capitalists. They said the capitalists were getting rich from the war while we were getting killed and maimed. And we were going around killing poor, innocent civilians who were the peace-loving peoples of the world.

In the beginning we didn't know what in hell they were talking about. We were standing there in the cold, too damn miserable to pay any attention. But after we got to Company 1, the lectures became more intense and we started to get reading material—newspapers, pamphlets, and magazines from China, Russia, Czechoslovakia and the United States. It was too much trouble for them to bring in decent food or medicine for us but they managed to get newspapers from the United States not more than a few weeks old.

I found it pretty rough to pick up a newspaper—*The Daily Worker* from New York or *The People's World* printed on the West Coast—and read how an English newspaper woman had visited the prison camps in Korea and seen how well we were being treated. She wrote that we were living in wonderful buildings, wearing good clothes the Chinese had issued us, and eating meat and eggs and fish three times a day. She said we had good medical care, sports facilities, and libraries filled with good

books. And all this time we were living in mud huts, sleeping on dirt floors, and getting eaten alive by the lice on the outside and the worms on the inside.

It would just make us feel damn bad and actually sick to have fought the Communists, to be prisoners of the Communists, to watch our friends die of mal-nutrition, to expect to die ourselves at any moment, and here were sons of bitches back in the United States, just as bad as the Communists, writing crap like that for the American people to read. Stuff that was nothing but a pack of made-up lies.

Since I was a monitor the Chinks would make me read certain articles to my squad. Then I would have to ask them questions about the articles and write down the answers and hand them in to headquarters. The monitor was in charge of all political matters in his squad and at first they picked them at random. Later they picked guys whose actions and opinions they liked and I didn't keep the job long.

We also had criticism meetings. Every man had to criticize himself or another man while the monitor took notes. It is a Communist trick to get information and to get you used to confessing or ratting. My squad stuck to things they didn't want to hear about. One man would say, "I'm John Smith. I criticize myself for not brushing my teeth this morning."

Then another guy would pipe up. "My name is Joe Blow. I criticize myself for not washing my teeth." Once we turned this in: "We criticize the Chinese Peoples Volunteers for not giving us tobacco, food, clothes and medical care." It wasn't what they liked, but they couldn't do anything about it because they said under Communism we could criticize anyone, as long as it was the truth. They did chew us out for making such a statement.

Late in May they started the indoctrination going full blast. There were lectures every day, hour after hour. They were about the Americans committing aggression in Korea, about soldiers being used for cannon fodder by the American imperialists, about racial discrimination at home, and about unemployment in the United States caused by Wall Streeters and monopolists.

At this time there were a lot of colored soldiers in Company 1 and the Chinks were really bearing down on racial discrimination. A few colored guys got up and said it was our business what we did in the United States and for the Chinks to mind their own damn business. Most of them wouldn't talk about racial discrimination and didn't say much.

After the lectures they would break us up into several groups and place one man in charge as the

discussion leader. He was supposed to lead the discussion, ask questions, and record answers along with the men's names. Some guys would listen to the question and say, "Go to hell." Others would agree with the Chinks. It was at this time that I noticed the prisoners were dividing into three groups.

There were the men who went along with the Chinese and agreed with everything they had to say. They stood up and publicly denounced their country, their government, all that America stood for, and their God. The Chinese called these men peace fighters and later they became known as progressives.

The largest group was in-between. These men were on the fence and didn't know which way to go. The Chinese got most of their information about what went on in the camp from this group. Not all of these men were bad. They had some damn good men in there, but some of them would denounce the Chinese to your face and sell you out behind your back.

Then there was the third group made up of men who were strictly against the Chinese—anything they said and anything they did. In the beginning these men were called stubborn students but later the Chinese said they were reactionaries.

The progressives were not Communists and they

didn't believe in Communism. It seemed to me that they had been protected all their lives. They always had someone they could run to and now the Chinese were their guardians. Whether or not they turned to the Communists for personal gain, I can't honestly say. They never got any big reward for anything they did—maybe a handful of peanuts or cigarettes, a few spoons of the food the Chinese didn't feel like eating, a few balls of hard candy, or a shirt some slopehead got tired of wearing. And yet for these measly things some of the progressives would have sold their souls.

A lot of people think these men were brainwashed, but it just isn't so. When they turned to the Chinks, the indoctrination had just started.

I was a reactionary because I was stubborn. I didn't like a guy to stand over me and preach things I knew were a pack of lies. I'm an American and I'm proud of it and I didn't like a Chink to try to tell me my government and my people were no damn good when they were a thousand times better than his. They said Americans were starving to death in the States and that we started the war—both lies. I spoke my mind when they said something like that so I was a reactionary. And I felt, as I did on the march when we were giving the Chinks the hip and knocking them off cliffs, that I was still an American soldier

and it was my duty to harass those bastards as much as possible. I had let my country down once by obeying an order to lay down my rifle and I damn sure wasn't going to have another time on my conscience.

There wasn't much anybody could do at this time except voice your opinions and contradict what the Communists said. One man, a skinny kid named Pritchett, had tried getting up at a company formation and telling the Chinks there was only one thing he was living for—to see Uncle Sam's tanks come rolling over the hills and run every damn Chink into the Yalu River.

He was immediately thrown under guard and taken to a small house up on a hill behind the camp. For a couple of days and nights we could hear him screaming. About three days later they brought him down and announced at formation that he had been attacked and killed by rats. I happened to get a look at the body and it was true he had been attacked by rats. You could tell they had been eating on him. But he also had a neat bullet hole right between his eyes.

About this time the Chinese decided they wanted to form a Central Peace Committee to draw up petitions. They planned to hold a big election in our camp. I was one of the men nominated in my com-

pany. The next day there was a company meeting and they wanted all the nominees to talk. The first four candidates said they would help the Chinese draw up petitions to help end the war sooner. When I got up, I told the men I would not ask them to sign anything un-American, or anything against the American government, or that the Chinese could use for propaganda purposes, or that could incriminate them when they got home. A colored man named Watson got up and said the same thing.

The Chinks got their heads together and said Watson and I had the wrong attitude and our names should be withdrawn. All the G.I.'s got mad and said we should run. The Chinks huddled again and said the camp commander had demanded that our names be withdrawn. And they just scratched them off the list of candidates. The G.I.'s got up and walked off the parade field, saying that if they couldn't vote the way they wanted, they weren't going to vote.

Watson and I were called into headquarters. They told us that if the men did not vote in the election, we would be shot. We went back to our squads. He told his men what the Chinks had said and asked them to vote. The men came to me and asked me what I wanted to do. I told them to decide for themselves, to do what they wanted. About 60 or 65 per

cent of the men voted. The Chinese relieved me of my job as monitor after that and sort of kept an eye on me.

Things began to get better in the camp. They came around and issued some clothes, soap, toothbrushes, and towels. We got some lime and made whitewash for the walls of our buildings. By this time we could also build fires to boil our clothes and get rid of the lice. There was enough food to keep us alive and I began putting on weight. I had been down to 85 or 90 pounds in April when I had dysentery. We stopped losing men in large numbers. One would die in the hospital now and then, but they were actually treating men there and they started to come back alive.

The indoctrination program was really rolling now. The Chinks had a "reactionary list" of unco-operative prisoners and I was on it. They forbade the men to hold religious services and took their Bibles away, saying that good Communists did not read such trash. The guys would ask them who the hell's professing to be a good Communist. Some of the Bibles had been issued by the Army and they had American flags printed inside the front cover. The guards would tear those pages out and hand back the Bibles. Some of the men would throw the Bibles back and say that,

by God, if they couldn't have it all, they didn't want any part of it.

In my squad I could argue against Communist ideas, but I couldn't do anything more. I had a few weaklings in there, men I couldn't trust to keep secrets from the Chinks. One of them was Scott L. Rush, of Marietta, Ohio, who decided to stay with the Chinese after the war was over. I don't know why he stayed. He didn't believe in Communism and he hadn't done anything in camp except ratting and writing some articles for the Chinese. He wouldn't have got in any trouble if he had come back because he wasn't as bad as some other men.

Rush was a friend of some of the big progressives and I didn't think any secret was safe with him. He also hung around with Gallagher, who was riding high then. Gallagher was a squad leader playing along with the Chinks. He agreed wholeheartedly with any and everything they said. I heard him say in a discussion that the Americans had aided the Japanese during the Second World War.

I approached him several times in Camp 5 and talked to him about the things he was doing and the men he had thrown out of his hut in the winter. He openly admitted them to me and told me flatly it was none of my Goddamned business what he did and

what he had done. He said he knew what he was doing and I told him, if we both got back to the States, I personally would see that he was hung.

Then without any warning the reactionaries got their first break. Cletys Nordin came up to me and said the Chinese had put a proposition to him. Before he had been captured, his wife had gone through a series of operations. He didn't know if she had pulled through or not. Now the Chinese had some of his letters from home. They told if he would play ball with them, they would give him his mail. It seemed that Cletys was well liked by the men and the Chinks felt they would stand a better chance with their indoctrination if they could get him on their side.

The Chinese had given Cletys a few hours to think it over and he wanted my advice. I had fought with him on the front lines and I had a lot of confidence in him. So I told him I had a plan to try to resist the brainwashing. A lot of men were beginning to weaken and my plan was to start a movement in my squad to keep the men straight. I told him it would be helpful to get him on the inside, to worm him into the confidence of the Chinese. He agreed to take the chance.

It was a pleasure to watch Cletys work. He just went ahead and played along with them, leading a

few discussions and writing some articles for them. If they said tit, he said tit. If they said tat, he said tat. He played it cool and kept his nose clean. Before long they were trusting him. They made him a monitor and that gave him a good excuse to go up to headquarters a lot.

Nordin kept us pretty well informed on the activities of the rats—who they were, what they were saying, and who they were saying it about. It wasn't long before we were able to make good use of this information.

Nine

AROUND the middle of October the Chinese told us that we would be shipped to Camp 3. They didn't say where it was or what we would do there. I can't say I was sorry to leave Camp 5 because we had suffered plenty and lost between 1,600 and 1,800 of our men there. Then on the 18th they marched us down to barges on the Yalu River. A motorized junk towed the barges to the new camp, about thirty-five miles southwest along the river.

We got to Camp 3 around three o'clock the next morning. It was raining and pretty cold. They moved us into the same kind of mud buildings we had at the last camp. That evening a couple of hundred men came in, skinny, ragged, and many of them barefooted even though it was sleeting at the time. They

were the survivors of the thousands of men the North Koreans had captured in the early days of the war and they looked like they were on their last legs. Of all the P.W.'s these men had the hardest time. They'd been eating grass, worms, grasshoppers, anything they could get their hands on. I saw them again a few months later and they looked like an entirely different group of men.

Everything went along about the same for a month, some of the men still playing along with the Chinks and some resisting them. One day in November a Chinese instructor named Wong, who was known as Sealed Beams or Goggle Eyes because of his thick eyeglasses, called ten of us up in front of a building. I knew some of the men and others I didn't. I had only heard about them.

Wong began by telling us what bad reactionaries we were. He said he thought that with a little more education we would be okay, and that the Chinese had decided to put us in a squad of our own. It would be known as the reactionary squad. I think the whole idea was supposed to shame us into becoming good Communists.

After the war the Army wanted to know how we had been able to form a reactionary squad inside a prison camp to give the enemy a hard time. The an-

swer was that we didn't form the squad—Wong and the other Chinks were dumb enough to do it for us.

After his little lecture, Wong assigned the squad to a room close to headquarters. He said they wanted to be able to observe our actions. I don't think he realized that we could keep an eye on headquarters and see who went in there. The last thing he did was appoint me squad leader and a kid named Vernon W. Clark, from Brooks, Maine, as monitor.

As soon as Wong left, we made an agreement that the squad would stick together and do everything we possibly could against the Chinese, regardless of the consequences. We also agreed that there would be no such thing as a leader. Before we would do anything, it would go up before a vote and the majority would rule. The squad that they called reactionary was run on democratic lines.

The squad began to get special attention from the Chinese. There was always an instructor with us when we had to discuss their lectures. In the other squads they left it up to the monitor. They called us up to headquarters a lot to see what they could learn from us, which wasn't much. And men were constantly trying to eavesdrop outside our squad room, trying to get information for the Chinks.

Looking back over the men in the reactionary

squad, I can see they had one thing in common. They all just hated the Chinese and weren't going to take indoctrination when it was rammed down their throats. The men weren't from any one part of the country and they had different backgrounds. They weren't highly educated and couldn't argue very much about politics, but they knew how a captured soldier should act.

There was Donnell Adams, from Cottonwood, Alabama, a six-foot country boy raised on a farm. He was stubborn as a mule when it came to giving in to the Chinese. Adams was about twenty-three then and he was a good soldier.

Frederick C. Gardner, Jr., came from Philadelphia. He was about six-three and had worked hard as a truck driver. He was easygoing until the Chinks got him mad and then all hell couldn't slow him down. He was twenty-six, the oldest of our group, and he had pulled patrol duty with the Army on the Austrian border. He'd seen the way the Russians acted over there and hated anything to do with them.

We had Willie J. Dorrill, from Troy, Alabama, who had lost seven of his toes due to the neglect of the Chinese. He had a personal grudge against them. Willie was a farm boy, about twenty-two then.

Then there was Milton H. Peters, from Powellton,

West Virginia, who had lost all his toes from frost-bite. He was about eighteen years old and weighed about 110 pounds, but he was all man and all soldier. I never found a man with more guts than that little guy had. No matter what you wanted to do against the Chinese, he was willing to do more than his share. He was an inspiration to all of us.

Alfred R. McMillan, from Sneads, Florida, was the quietest of the whole squad. Mac never said much, just mostly listened. When he did say something, you knew it was the truth and had sound logic behind it. He was quite a soldier.

Vernon Clark had been a lumberjack back in Maine. He didn't like to have people trying to cram something down his throat, trying to make him believe stuff that he knew was a damn lie. Clark was about five-seven, dark haired and weighed 135 pounds.

There was also Preston J. Hibbard, from Harlan, Kentucky, who was about twenty-four then and weighed about 150 pounds. He had seen what the Chinks had done in the other prison camps and had one of the biggest hates for them among any of the men.

We had two other G.I.'s in the squad with us. I won't name them because they know who they are.

They weren't with us. We never actually knew for a fact that these men were rats, but one went to headquarters almost every night. Why, I don't know. He was always scared and reminded me of a cornered rat. The other man just wasn't willing to buck up against the Chinese the way he should have. Sometimes we made them do things along with us so the Chinks would consider them as guilty as us.

When the reactionary squad was formed, the men in Camp 3 were feeling the brainwashing. The Chinese had damn near full control of the whole company of 342 men. It was at the place that you didn't know who to trust. We started to work in the discussion meetings because we had the right to talk there. The whole squad would stick together and argue against every statement the Chinese would make.

If a G.I. stood up and sided with the Chinese, we would shame him right in front of all the men. Even though the instructors were there, we would still shame him. We'd ask him what kind of damn soldier did he think he was to stand there and side with his enemy—people he had fought and who were still fighting against his country.

Most of the men we shamed would just hang their heads, sit down, and shut up. But there were a few of the big boys like Gallagher and James G. Veneris,

a turncoat who stayed with the Chinks, who would stand up and argue with you as though they meant it. These were the men who really did the damage to the minds of the other prisoners.

Even though the open progressives gave us a lot of trouble at the discussions, we weren't too concerned about them. We knew them and we knew what they were up to. It was the quiet man, the man who never took any side, the man who would eavesdrop on you and run to the Chinese, that we were worried about. Every man in the squad except Donnell Adams and me considered Cletys Nordin a progressive. That's the way we wanted it. He had got himself in good with the Chinks and was finding out about the quiet progressives for us.

One day Gallagher and some other progressives and the Chinks came around with two petitions for us to sign. One was a letter to Mao Tse-tung thanking him for the lenient treatment we were getting. The other was to some committee back in the States asking them to put pressure on the government to end the war. My squad told them to go to hell.

They took their petitions down the street to another squad and Milton Peters went after them. He snatched the petitions out of a Chink's hands and tore them up. That's when the trouble started. They took

Peters up to headquarters and stood him at attention for a long time in the cold and snow. They threatened to shoot him. He told them they were a bunch of chicken-livered sons of bitches if they didn't shoot him.

The Chinks marched the rest of the squad to a lecture hall where Wong hollered at us. He said we were a big bunch of imperialist agents, trying to sabotage the people's studies and fighting against the peace-loving peoples of the world. He also thought we were secret agents who had got captured to disrupt the studies and spy on the students. In general he was highly displeased at our conduct. He said if we kept it up we would never go home.

When he finished talking to us, they had taken Peters away and we didn't know what had happened to him.

These instructors were the screwiest bunch of characters I ever saw. They were the best educated, the cream of the crop, and they thought of themselves as great psychologists. But all they ever used on us was simple bribery. In other words, if you'll be good, I'll give you some candy. They were so narrow-minded that they couldn't run the camp right.

One day they lined up the company for a big surprise shakedown. They were looking for knives, which

we made from old pieces of iron. All they could find was marijuana. It grew wild in the camp and they found over a bushel on us. They just looked at it and handed it back. The next day they held another surprise inspection. They were looking for marijuana this time. And all they could find was knives, knives of every size and shape. So they gave the knives back to us.

There was another instructor named Wong. We called this one Ragmop because his hair was six inches long and stood up like a porcupine's. He was so cockeyed he was the only man I've seen who could look in three directions at the same time. Ragmop caught me tearing a board off a building to help start a fire. He stood me at attention and chewed me up one side and down the other. He called me all kinds of American imperialist and warmonger. Finally I got mad and called him a slant-eyed son of a bitch. He dismissed me. Two weeks later he called me into headquarters and asked me, "Pate, why did you call me a slant-eyed son of a bitch?" It took two weeks for it to dawn on him that he had been insulted.

The Chinese let us celebrate Thanksgiving that year. They gave us a few chickens, a little pork, some peanuts and cigarettes and candy. The same thing happened at Christmas. New Year's wasn't as big but

the meal was still nice compared to what we had been eating. Donnell Adams took it upon himself to go to the kitchen and steal some oil so we could have a light to celebrate by.

Adams had a hard time stealing the oil. It was in a fifty-five gallon drum and he had to tip it to fill our small bowl. He spilled it all over and left a perfect trail of oil in the snow back to our door. The next day the assistant company commander came following that oil like a bloodhound after a convict. He traced it to our door and went to headquarters for a bunch of instructors. As soon as he left one of our guys threw the oil we had left up the fireplace.

The instructors came and wanted one or all of us to confess stealing the oil. Nobody said a word. We just didn't know what they were talking about. They started searching and one Chink stuck his hand up the fireplace. It came out all oily. Then they said they would punish the whole squad if the guilty man didn't admit it. Adams said he did it and they took him away and put him into a bomb shelter, which was a covered hole in the ground.

A few instructors came back for me and said they would punish me as squad leader because I had not ratted on Adams. They took me to a small supply shack near the bomb shelter. There was a four-foot

hole underneath it where the Chinks used to throw their wash water and they put me in it. They put me in about seven in the morning and the weather was about thirty below. About an hour and a half later, my platoon leader, who was known as Rubberlips, came by. "Pate, are you cold?" he asked.

"Hell, no," I told him. He ordered me to give him my cotton padded jacket and left with it. Half an hour later he was back and wanted to know if I was cold. I said no and he took my shoes. He came back for the third time to play the game some more and took my pants. So there I was completely naked at thirty below zero and feeling sorry as hell for myself.

A little later Rubberlips and an instructor named Wu called me out. They said if I'd write a confession, they would give me my clothes and let me go back to the squad. I told them I had nothing to confess and got back into the hole without giving them the satisfaction of telling me to.

Some of our friends heard about Adams and me being in the hole. They rolled extra-big cigarettes, lit them and threw them down to us. It began to get cold as hell and my feet started to freeze. I massaged them and they didn't freeze up, but I lost my toenails again. A G.I. cook came by and I told him to send me some hot peppers with chow that night. He sent them

all right, but Adams got them. He knew I liked peppers and began joking about them. "Boy, they sure were good," he shouted over. "I'm over here sweating like hell."

Shortly after that Rubberlips brought my clothes back. When I put them on it was like walking into a steam-heated building. I never thought clothes could feel so good. Around eleven-thirty that night the Chinks took us from the holes, stood us at attention for thirty minutes and chewed us out. They made us criticize ourselves and promise it wouldn't happen again and sent us back to the squad.

It was around this time that I met Gallagher in the street. He was really going along with the Chinks in any way he could and I asked him what in the hell did he think he was doing. I told him he already had the blood of some men on his hands and didn't he think that was enough. I said it still wasn't too late to try to make amends for what he had done. He told me to mind my own damn business, that it wasn't any concern of mine.

So I asked him if he didn't know that the American government was going to rack his behind when he got home. He said he wasn't worried because all he had to do was plead that he had done everything under mental duress. Duress, hell, I told him, he was as sane

as I was and there'd be a hundred guys who'd get up and testify to it. We had a little debate on law then, a subject that neither of us knew a damn thing about, and I finally got mad and walked away.

My squad was pretty busy now, going around to the men and talking to them. We knew about articles these men had written for the Chinese. The articles were pro-Communist, about aggression and atrocities and biological warfare in Korea with all the blame on the Americans. All we could do was take these men aside, talk to them, shame them privately. A lot of these men straightened out.

Late in February the Chinese decided that the reactionary squad was too close to headquarters and could spy on the men reporting in. They moved us down by the riverbank to an empty building that was more than one hundred yards from the nearest G.I.'s. It was the biggest mistake they made.

Ten

THE more we looked at the new squad building the better we liked it. Not only was it away from the rest of the camp, but it was hard to get to. The path to our building came straight down an embankment twenty feet high and nobody could sneak up on us. We found that we had a nice quiet place to do some brainwashing of our own.

There was a kid who worked with the Chinese in headquarters. The first thing we did was call him in and put a proposition to him. He had been pretty pink. We told him if he would help us and do what we wanted, we would help him back in the States if the government ever tried to prosecute him.

I am not going to mention the name of this kid we had in headquarters because I don't want to cause

him any embarrassment. He straightened out and turned out to be one hell of a man. He was sick and was always passing out from what I thought were heart attacks, but he took plenty of chances. He was the most valuable man in our organization.

The main thing we wanted this kid to do was keep his eyes and ears open when G.I.'s came in to headquarters to report to the Chinks. We wanted to know who was ratting and what they were saying. We also wanted him to steal articles that the men had written for the Communists. And to get any other information he thought would be helpful. It wasn't long before this kid was delivering everything we wanted.

Now every time the kid or Cletys Nordin would get the name of a rat or of an article writer we would go to talk to the man. We would try to show them where they were messing up. Some of these men would admit the things they had written were damn lies and would start flying right. We gave each man two private talks before we gave up on that tactic.

Just talking didn't seem to do any good for some of the men. So we would get them down at our squad and beat the hell out of them. We would send word to these men that we wanted to see them at the squad and most would show up. When they didn't, we'd drag them down. As far as we knew none of the men

ever told the Chinks about a beating. Most of them straightened out and became soldiers America could be proud of. Some we had to work over twice before they realized we meant what we said.

There was one particular individual in the company who enjoyed himself by getting up at formations and reading some Communist lectures. We straightened him out real quick by telling him if he didn't stop it he'd find himself floating face down in the river one morning. He became one of the biggest reactionaries in the company. The Chinks would tell him to do something and instead of jumping to it like he did before, he'd tell them to go to hell.

A lot of the men we beat up told us about other rats that we didn't know of. That gave us the opportunity to work them over and get them behaving also.

There were about eighteen or twenty Mexican boys in the company. Most of them were pretty damn good guys, but there were exceptions. We brought three of the Mexican boys into our little organization to help them keep the rest of their men in line. Another kid named Adair, who was called Peanut because of his small size, joined our group and helped us.

The Chink indoctrination program came to a dead stop. They couldn't hold a decent company formation. They couldn't do a damn thing. Everybody was

afraid to move except guys who didn't have anything to hide. We told the guys not to fall out for lectures unless the Chinks got guns and forced them to go. At the lectures they did hold, even former progressives wouldn't agree with anything the Chinks said.

The big pros were beginning to sweat. We didn't try talking to them or working them over because those guys were too far gone and they would have run to the Chinks. They got to be a little leery of doing what the Chinese said, but they kept on doing it even if they didn't like it. None of them knew exactly how far we would go. I think a lot of them expected to wake up one morning with their throats cut.

We started taking nails up to the road at night and burying them with the points up. Then when the Chinese trucks and convoys would come through they'd have flats. We held several small convoys up for a few days. I remember one poor bastard who had eleven flats in a hundred feet. As fast as he'd fix one and ride a few feet, he'd blow out another tire.

The Chinks got pretty wise to this. They never made any public announcement but they started posting guards with rifles in positions where they could watch the road. Then we started making gadgets out

of nails and wire. These things didn't have to be planted. We'd just drop them and they always landed with three points down and one point up. Every morning when we went for our trot, someone would scatter a few of the gadgets on the road.

By this time the Chinks were going crazy. They didn't know what in hell had happened or who was behind it, but they knew they didn't have their old control over our company and they didn't like it. They had a general idea that the reactionary squad was to blame but they couldn't prove a thing.

Several times men came to the squad for help when they wanted to escape. We would steal maps, food, knives and other things for them. We could tell the men the exact time the guards would pass a certain point, when the sergeant of the guard came around checking, and when they relieved the guard. Some escapes were cut off short when the progressives got wind of it and told the Chinks. The men would be thrown in an old bomb shelter called the hole for a few days, would pull a few weeks' hard labor, and would have to write criticisms.

None of the escapes was successful, but at least we could say we tried. It wasn't too hard to get out of camp, but from then on it got rough. The Chinks would search the immediate vicinity and then they

would put out an alarm. The North Koreans would keep their eyes open because there was a reward for every prisoner they brought back.

In this one escape a kid named David E. Fortune gave me his personal papers and pictures to hold. In case he got killed in trying to escape, I was to try to get the papers back to his people in Pickens, South Carolina. Dave went with a boy named Smitty and they got four days out of camp, which was a good try for that area. When they were brought back, the Chinks beat the hell out of them, but nothing serious happened.

At the height of our reactionary program, a Chinese instructor named Ling came for me and took me to his office in headquarters. He put his finger to his lips, motioning me to be quiet and then he motioned me to sit down on the floor. I was completely befuddled. There were offices on each side of his, separated by paper walls.

A few minutes later I heard some people come into the office on my left. I recognized the voice of Wong, the instructor we called Sealed Beams. He said, "Sit down here, Gallagher." They started talking. At first it was a general bull session: How are you doing? How is the chow? Have you heard from home lately? Stuff like that.

Then Wong asked him, "What seems to be wrong with the studies?"

Gallagher just sort of laughed. "You mean to say you don't know what's going on?" he said. "Everybody going around with busted mouths and noses and you're wondering what's happened to the studies."

"We have seen them and we have an idea what is going on," Wong said. "And we have an idea who is behind it. But we want to be sure and we want to hear about it from you students."

"Well," Gallagher said, "all I can say is that the progressive students in the company are being beat up and threatened by Pate and his squad. Or I would be willing to bet it is them. As long as Pate and his men are permitted to do what they're doing, you'll never be able to put over your studies."

Wong then asked him what he would suggest they do with me and my men.

"If I was in your place," Gallagher said, "I'd take Pate out and shoot him. And if necessary, his men, too."

They started talking about a few other things and then got around to my squad again. Wong started calling off the names of the men in the squad and Gallagher was giving him advice. Two other times

in the conversation Gallagher made the statement that if he had the authority, he'd have me and my men shot.

When they got on a general bull session again, Ling motioned me to go outside with him. We got up very quietly and went out. We were standing a few yards from the building when Wong and Gallagher came out. They saw me and Gallagher's mouth dropped open and Wong's eyes got bigger than his glasses. He walked over to Ling and they started talking in Chinese. He must have got a satisfactory answer because he went back to Gallagher and they both walked away.

I never mentioned the incident to Gallagher because he'd probably have run to Wong and got Ling in a hell of a lot of trouble. And I never found out why Ling let me hear that conversation. A lot of guys said Ling was queer. I know he took a fancy to me, but he never made any advances and I never heard any G.I. say he made any advances. Why he liked me, I don't know. He used to take me aside and ask me a lot of questions about the Bible. Maybe he was trying to get religion.

The whole squad had more or less expected one of the big pros to squeal on us. I knew that sooner or later the Chinese were going to catch up with us.

But we believed that if we could set an example for the meatheads in the company, maybe they would perk up and start acting like soldiers. We all knew there was a chance that if we ever got caught, we'd be taken out and shot with no questions asked. But we felt it was a worth-while cause.

All told we talked to 75 to 100 men out of the 342 men in the company and there were a hell of a lot more that needed to be talked to. We beat up a couple of dozen men, maybe a little more. After Gallagher's talk with Wong, we started working on the men harder than before so we would do as much as we could before they finally caught up with us.

A few days later the Chinks started cracking down on my squad. At first they worked on the whole company, calling us out several times a day and making us go to formations. The fallouts weren't for lectures, they were for shakedowns. They said they were looking for knives and marijuana, but they weren't. Then they started leaving the company alone and concentrated on my squad. They'd fall us out all hours of the day and night, throw our stuff out in the yard, and just tear it up in general.

They finally came out in the open and told us they knew we had stolen papers from headquarters and they wanted them right back. We just laughed at

them. They got pretty damn indignant about it. What they didn't know was that the papers were buried less than three feet from where they were standing in our yard. They kept calling us up to headquarters and said that if we would confess and criticize ourselves in front of the company, all would be forgotten. We'd tell them we didn't know what they were talking about and they'd dismiss us. When we got back to the squad all our gear would be lying in the slush and mud.

On April 11, a Chink we called Slim called me out of the squad, pulled his pistol, and took me to headquarters. Warped Jaw, the assistant regimental commander, and a Chinese intelligence officer were there. Warped Jaw said they knew all about my activities, how I was leading a small band of men against the Chinese and the peace-loving peoples. He said he knew all about the stolen papers. They were so anxious to get those papers because in some of them G.I.'s had ratted on other men.

Warped Jaw said that if I would give the papers back and get my squad to stop its activities, he would forget about what we had done. But if I didn't, it was very likely we would not be going home when the war was over. I told him I was very sorry I couldn't help him out. Real polite like. I said I didn't

know a thing about it. He got a little nasty and said he was going to send me down to regimental head-quarters to give me time to think about my crimes.

I was marched out under guard and told that if I talked to anybody I would be severely punished. This was a crock of bull because I spoke to several men on the way down. When I got there they put me into a little sentry shack, about five by five. I didn't know it then but I'd never see the recactionary squad intact again and my part in its work was over.

Eleven

AFTER I sat in the sentry shack for a few hours, the Chinese came for me and took me to a building used as quarters for the officer of the guard. It had one room fixed up for special prisoners and they told me to get in there.

A G.I. was sitting on the porch in front of the room, a man I had never seen before. I sat down before him and introduced myself. He turned out to be from the West, a big man about six-one and weighing 190 pounds. I was suspicious of any man who weighed that much in a prison camp because it meant he had been eating too well.

The man told me we were in segregation and said we could come and go as we pleased as long as we didn't try to speak to the other men. He asked me

what I had done to get put in segregation and I said, nothing. We just sat there and had a bull session. Every once in a while he'd sneak in a question about what I had done. Each time I'd tell him, nothing. He didn't press the matter too much.

I was treated better, ate better, and was left alone more in segregation than at any other time as a prisoner. We didn't have to work, but we would help the Chinese in the kitchen just for exercise. We would carry water for the cooks, cut wood for fires, and help them clean their vegetables.

Three days after I arrived in segregation, we were chopping wood near a G.I. labor company when I saw Milton Peters sneaking away from his detail and crawling over to us. I hadn't seen him since he tore up the Chinese peace petition and I was happy as hell he was alive. Peters pointed at my roommate and ran his finger across his throat. That meant my hunch was right; the man was a known rat and had been put in my room for a purpose.

The labor company guards begun to get a little suspicious and were looking around for Peters. I started singing "You'd Better Run to the City of Refuge," an old religious song, and he took off. After that he would slip me notes, tobacco, and other things I needed whenever he got a chance.

A few times the Chinese dropped in on me and asked me to confess my activities. They told me that some of my men had already confessed. I knew better because none of my men would rat. So I told them that if any men in the squad had confessed, he had confessed to a lie. The Chinese didn't like it, but they left it at that.

One day I was in the room looking at the papers Dave Fortune had left with me when he tried his escape. My roommate came in and saw me looking at them. He asked me what they were. I put the papers in my pocket and told him none of his business. The next day the officer of the guard and a Chinese instructor came to our room for a search.

They searched the room and then searched us. It took them five minutes to go through my friend's stuff and an hour and a half to search me and my gear. They found Dave's papers and the instructor wanted to know where I'd got them. I said Fortune was a buddy of mine who got killed on the front lines and I was saving the papers to take home to his family. He took the papers to headquarters and checked up. They found out I was lying, but I wouldn't admit it and they let the matter drop.

Everything went along pretty smooth for a few weeks. Then they sent in a man from my old com-

pany, also a man from the West. He wasn't an open progressive, but I had never trusted him. The two of them started to try to get information from me but a rat is not dangerous if you know him for what he is and I didn't tell them anything. After forty-eight days the Chinks saw that they weren't going to learn anything from me through these men and they decided to send me to the labor company. Before they let me go, old Warped Jaw talked to me through an interpreter. It was the same old stuff about the peace-loving Chinese and the Wall Street imperialist warmongers. I was used to this speech by now, but when he kept it up for a good thirty minutes, I lost my temper. I told the interpreter to tell the warped-jawed, slant-eyed, slope-headed son of a bitch that if he had nothing else to talk to me about to either put me back in segregation or send me to the company.

When the interpreter got through telling him what I said, Warped Jaw started turning colors. He shook his finger at me and tried to say something, but he couldn't. I thought my big mouth had got me in trouble again, but Warped Jaw just walked out. The interpreter was white as a sheet. "The assistant regimental commander is very mad," he said. Then they just shipped me to the labor company.

I found Peters right away and he let me in on the lowdown on who to trust and who not to trust. It turned out that there were very few safe men in the company. When I told him what we had been up to in the reactionary squad, he just laughed. I never saw a man so damn happy over the way we had messed up the progressives.

Peters and I started planning an escape. We brought a third man in with us. He was Abner Alfred, Jr., from Speedway, Indiana. Alfred was a very loud-mouthed person and he hated the Chinks with a passion. When he started talking you could hear him a block away. But he could keep a secret and he had a hell of a lot of guts.

We began to save food and make knives and maps. After a while we managed to get some Army fatigues. They were handy for escapes because they were green and were good cover in the hills. We planned to get into an empty building about a hundred yards from the barracks. There was a deep ditch behind it, leading down to the river, and we figured we could get out of camp that way.

In the middle of June we were ready to go. We planned to get into the empty building one by one. Alfred went first and made it. There never was a guard in front of the building, but the Chinks had got

wind of our plan and stopped us cold. They suddenly threw a guard in front of the building and it
was impossible for Peters and me to join Alfred. He
hid his provisions under a rock in the floor and calmly
walked back toward the company. The Chinks
grabbed him, took him to headquarters, and turned
him loose after a few hours.

When we went back into the building a few days
later to look for the provisions, they were gone. The
Chinks seemed to know everything that was going on
in that company. So we had to start all over again.

By the 28th of June we were ready again. The night
was dark and it was raining like hell. No sooner had
we left the barracks than all the guards started flash-
ing lights around. They were looking every place for
us. It was obvious that a rat had seen us put on fatigues and had tipped off the Chinks. We hid in the
grass and when they got too close we threw rocks
over to the other side of them and they went to investigate the sounds.

Finally we sneaked through two different company
areas and reached the main road. We crossed it and
got out of camp up into the hills. We walked up
one hill and down another. All that night and until
well after daylight the next morning we walked.
Then we hid in the brush. We tried to build a shelter

out of sticks, but it wasn't any good. It was still raining and our food, tobacco, and matches got wet.

At this time we weren't over three miles from the camp. By staying in the hills we had walked all night without getting far. The footing was treacherous and we never knew when we were going to walk over a cliff. In the morning we could see the whole layout of the terrain from our position. We had to make a choice—either follow the ridge line around, which would take several days, or walk down into the valley and up the other hill, which would take a few hours. Time was an important factor. We knew the Chinks would send up searching parties before long and we had to get out of there real fast, or else. We knew the shorter route through the valley was more dangerous, but we didn't see any houses down there and thought we had a reasonable chance of making it.

That night, when it got good and dark, we took off. We got down into the valley and followed the road for a few hundred yards. As we came around a sharp bend in the road, we saw a house sitting there. Koreans were sitting on the porch and out in the yard. They saw us and we stuck out like sore thumbs. We couldn't stop—we had to keep walking and try to bluff our way through. It didn't work. The Koreans

grabbed knives and sickles and ran out to surround us.

There were about a dozen of them. They searched us and took our knives and food and salt. Then they had a conference among themselves and started marching us back toward the camp. A few hours later we were back in front of headquarters. The Chinks came out and looked at us. For some reason they singled Alfred out and put handcuffs on him. Then they threw us into a room. There were G.I.'s in the rooms on either side of us, but we didn't know who they were.

That morning I punched a hole through one mud wall and found that Donnell Adams was in the next room. He told me what had happened after I left the squad. The men had kept on beating up progressives and rats, disrupting the studies, and giving the Chinks a hard time in general. Then the Chinks started pulling the men out, one by one, and throwing them into solitary. Adams told me somebody had confessed. He didn't know who, but the man had pinpointed me as the leader and him as next in command. Adams didn't have much time to talk to me because the guards kept checking on us. Soon they came and took me to another room.

All I can say about the cell in which they threw

me in solitary is that I spent the worst part of my captivity there. It was a small room, about nine feet by nine, with no windows in the mud walls. The door was boarded up and no sunlight could come in. They put me in on June 30, and when I got out on August 4 my hair had turned gray even though I was only eighteen years old. Later it turned dark again.

For about eighteen hours a day I had to sit cross-legged on the floor with my back straight. It was painful to sit like that and my knees still tell me about it. When the guard came to check on me, he'd poke me with the butt of his rifle or with his bayonet if I'd changed the position of my legs. They checked on me every fifteen minutes. After a while I learned to watch for the guard's shadow through the cracks in the door. Then I could lay down and relax until I saw him coming. But this cat-and-mouse game finally got me. Even when I was permitted to sleep, I couldn't because every time the guard came to check, I would automatically sit up and cross my legs.

After three or four days of this, they called me up to headquarters. There sat my old instructor Ragmop and an officer who said he was a criminal intelligence man. "Pate, we want you to confess to four things," Ragmop said. "Number one, what? Number two,

what? Number three, what? And number four, what?"

I looked at him and didn't know what in hell was coming off. "Let me get this straight," I said. "You want me to confess to four things?"

"That's right," Ragmop said.

"Number one, what? Two, what? Three, what? And four, what?" I asked.

"That's right," Ragmop said again. He seemed pleased that I was catching on.

"What in the hell is what" I asked.

"That's what we want you to confess to," he said.

"To what?" I shouted.

"That's it," he said.

I looked at the criminal intelligence man and told him if he wanted me to confess, he'd better get some-one in there with the common sense to tell me what he wanted. Ragmop said I had the wrong attitude and was being hostile. He put me in handcuffs and sent me back to solitary.

They left me there about six days with my arms handcuffed behind my back. It was miserable. They took them off only at chow time and to let you go to the latrine. It was torture to lie down and try to sleep. After a time my shoulders felt like they were going to fall off. Every once in a while I would walk through

the handcuffs and get them in front of me, but then a guard would come in and put them back on behind me a little tighter than before.

Finally they brought me down to headquarters again. There was a different interpreter. He told me they wanted me to confess and he left me alone with some writing paper and a pen. From what Adams told me and from the questions the Chinks had asked, I knew someone had spilled it all and the Chinks knew as much about the squad as I did. There wasn't any point in being stubborn any more. The longer I held out, the longer I was going to be miserable in that damn solitary.

I sat down and wrote them a seventeen-page confession. Everything that had gone on in the company was in there, but I left out all the names. I said I was the leader all the time, that I had instigated everything that happened, and that I was to be held responsible, not the men who did what I told them to. While I was writing the confession, I stole a big sheet of paper and a pencil lead and hid them on me.

The Chinks put me back in solitary without my handcuffs. I sat down and wrote practically word for word what I had put in my confession. By this time almost the whole squad was in solitary and we were

using the same latrine. I told the guard I had to go there and I left the paper, some cigarettes and matches, and a note to the guys telling them to make their stories jibe with mine. As far as I know everybody confessed to the same thing.

It got so rough in solitary that I thought I was going out of my mind. I had too much time to think about my people, whether my mother and father and grandmother were dead, whether I'd ever see them. No matter how hard I tried, my mind always came back to them.

I started wondering whether I was going to be taken out and shot. And I started thinking about the company, the way the men were sticking up for the Chinese. And the way they had turned on one another and sold out their country. It reminded me of a bunch of hungry little kids at a birthday party trying to get to the cake and ice cream before the other kids did. Only here they were trying to see who could tell the Chinese the most on the other men and who could write the best pro-Communist articles just to get a pat on the back from the Chinese.

It got to the point where I found a nail and would scratch myself with it because it would hurt and relieve some of the tension on my mind. When the guard came in and jabbed me in the legs with his

bayonet, it was welcome because the pain got my mind off the worries that were driving me crazy.

Then on August 4, thirty-six days after they threw me in solitary, the Chinks came and said they were going to court-martial fourteen of us. That was the whole squad, the three Mexican boys, and Peanut Adair. They advised me not to say a word in the courtroom and said every word I did speak would add six months to my sentence.

The trial took place that day and was funny in some ways. I think they were afraid of us. They marched us to a schoolhouse which was the trial room. All around the building they had vehicles parked with machine guns, Bren guns, Browning automatic rifles, carbines, and other weapons on them. They even had dug in machine guns. And we were fourteen sick, skinny, unarmed G.I.'s. Maybe they expected us to start World War III. I don't know.

In the courtroom there were over a hundred guards with everything from an Army .45 to a .30-caliber machine gun. About a hundred G.I.'s were there as spectators. They had a trial board, a prosecutor, and a defense counsel. The minute we arrived they started right in reading the charges against us. There were sixty-seven charges against my name and it took ten minutes to read them. Apparently I was guilty of

sabotage, espionage, beating up progressive students, instigating the smoking of marijuana (which was a lie), stealing documents and other things.

As soon as they finished reading the charges, they started sentencing. During the trial our defense counsel never spoke a word. All he did was sit there and laugh. I received a year at hard labor and Adams got the same. The other men got sentences ranging from nine months down to three months and three men were turned loose to go back to the company.

It wasn't a court-martial—a kangaroo court was all it was. We were already found guilty and sentenced before we went in there. I don't know why they went through all that formality and trouble when it would have been simpler to come around and say I was sentenced to a year at hard labor.

After the trial, we were sent back to the guard building and all put in three rooms. You can't imagine how good it felt to be able to sit around and talk again. We sat around, did a little work like cutting wood and unloading barges, and ate our chow. Once they sent us across the river to string communication lines, but I guess we were just plain bad because we started sabotaging the peace-loving Chinks again.

All they had were two guards to keep an eye on us. When they weren't looking, we would take the

wire and break it with rocks. Then we would fix the insulation so it looked pretty good and string the wire. From the ground it looked like a good line.

We strung two miles of wire that way but the Chinks never got a message through that line.

The guards weren't too careful about how they treated us. A few times they pulled us out of our building and roughed us up. They used to like to make us stare at the sun for thirty or forty minutes, but you'd be a damn fool if you did stare at it. All you had to do was look to one side, and all they'd do was kick your shins if they caught you. Other times they made a kid kneel on a rock and piled more rocks on him. Some kids got beaten with a stick. They had no policy—it depended on how the guards felt. One day a guard would give you tobacco, matches, anything you wanted. The next day he'd beat the hell out of you.

On September 9, the guards came and got six of us—Adams, Gardner, Peters, and me from the re-actionary squad; Alfred, who had escaped with us and pulled seventy-two days in handcuffs for it, and a kid from Pennsylvania who the Chinks just didn't like. They loaded us in a truck and said we were going to jail. We wouldn't have believed it then, but it was our first step toward home.

Twelve

THE truck ride to jail took most of the day. Late in the afternoon we arrived at Camp 2, which was northwest of Pyoktong and our old Camp 5. A couple of Chinese searched us and took all our G.I. clothing away. Then they took us to the jail, an old mud building with guards around it. It was several hundred yards away from the nearest P.W.'s.

When we got inside we found some Englishmen in there. We spoke to them, asking how they were doing and how everything was. They wouldn't answer. They just looked at us. At first we thought England was mad at the United States. We spoke again and they still wouldn't answer. So finally we asked them what was wrong. "You aren't supposed to talk in jail," one of them whispered.

We tried to change their minds, but they said if you got caught talking it was hard to tell what would happen to you. We told them it was worth while talking even if a few of us got stood at attention and beaten up. But they just couldn't see it. So we said that, by God, if the Englishmen could live without talking, we could too. We sat like a bunch of dumb wooden Indians looking at each other. It was a very unnatural life for a G.I.

Almost every day we were called out to do some kind of work. The ration details were the worst. We had to walk about eight miles to the Yalu River to unload barges and then bring the food back. It was getting pretty cold by this time. Once when we went up in the hills to get wood, my feet got frostbitten. I lost my toenails again and the soles of both feet. I hate to think how many toenails I left all over Korea.

The food in the jail was about as bad as when we were first captured. All we were getting was sorghum and we began to lose weight. Occasionally the G.I.'s in the regular P.W. company who cooked our jail chow would hide a can of tobacco in the food, but they didn't have much to spare and couldn't do it too often.

Early in December the Chinks brought in a group of men from Camp 1. A better bunch I never met

anywhere. As they came through the door they were talking and laughing and giving the Chinks a hard time. We all started talking and never stopped. The guards tried to make us shut up but the men from Camp 1 just told them to go to hell. Even the Englishmen began to talk. All the men from Camp 1 had tobacco, as much as five packages each, and for the first time in over six months we could roll a cigarette, smoke it, and enjoy it without worrying about where the next one would come from.

The jail got pretty crowded and the Chinese started sending men back to their companies. Pretty soon Adams and I were the only two left from the group that had come from Camp 3. We continued to work and pull our details.

One evening, after we hadn't had any decent food for over three weeks, a Korean pig came into the yard. She'd had piglets about two weeks before and they were still hanging on her tits. We decided to snatch one of the little pigs and one of the men ran into the yard and got one without being seen by the guards.

There was a kitchen in the building with a fireplace and one pot, but before we could do anything about the pig, a Chink guard came in to make his usual check. An Englishman named Derek grabbed the

pig and jumped under a blanket with it. The guard looked at Derek and asked what was wrong with him. We said he was a little sick and the guard walked on. When Derek came from under the blanket, we found he had smothered the pig while he was trying to keep it quiet.

We boiled the little pig and ate him. He was so young that his bones were soft and we ate them along with the rest of him. It was a good thing we did because the next day the Koreans and the guards came looking for the missing pig. They were suspicious of us and raised hell about American imperialists stealing from the peace-loving people of Korea. But they couldn't prove anything because we had eaten all the evidence.

At the beginning of May the Chinks just changed overnight. They came in and issued soap and towels, a shirt, a summer uniform, tobacco, toothbrushes and powder, razors and blades, and even a little mirror. We didn't know what in hell was coming off. Our food picked up and I went from 140 pounds to 170 pounds in six weeks. Later we figured out that it all had been caused by Operation Little Switch, when both sides repatriated the sick and wounded. The Chinks expected the war to end pretty soon. We were a sad-looking crew and they wanted to fatten us up.

Those of us still left in jail on the 5th of June were loaded on a truck and moved to another camp about halfway to Pyoktong and up in the hills. We were placed in another jail, two heavily guarded rooms in a compound in which Koreans still were living. This was a mystery camp and I never found out what it was or who was in it. The other prisoners in the camp were about seven hundred yards away from us and we never got close to them. Our food turned to slop again and we started to lose weight.

After three weeks in that camp the Chinese came around and said they were letting five of us out of jail. On June 25 we got on a truck and went to Pyok-tong, where we spent the night. The next day three of the men were sent to Camp 5, one went to Camp 3, and I drew Camp 1. I was assigned to a platoon and squad and I stayed there, just keeping my nose clean, until the armistice was signed.

Camp 1 was the softest touch of the war. We were fed three times a day and received meat once a day. After what I was used to, the food was so rich that sometimes I couldn't eat. The Chinks were friendly as hell when I got there. They had a public-address system set up in the company area and played American records a couple of times a day. The men had no room for complaint at this time.

With all the soft treatment, I'd have thought the progressives wouldn't try to butter up the Chinese. But they did. I had plenty of time to watch them and their activities. They came and went as they pleased, in and out of the company areas. They thought nothing about going to regimental headquarters and making pro-Communist broadcasts or voice recordings. For one of these they would receive 175,000 Chinese dollars and come back bragging about it. The money was enough to buy a couple of cartons of cigarettes, peanuts, and candy in the Chinese commissary, which the progressives were permitted to use.

I was tempted more than once to try to do something about these progressives, but I had just finished pulling a year in jail and I felt that the war was just about over. So I just minded my own damn business and didn't have too much to say to anybody.

On the 27th of July the Chinks called the whole camp to regimental headquarters. They told us the good news—the armistice had been signed at ten o'clock that morning and it went into effect at ten that night. They said we all would be going home soon. It seemed that we had been waiting for this for so damn long that it couldn't be real. But in a few days the American Red Cross came in and issued

good old American cigarettes, soap, towels, razors, and toothbrushes. Then we knew the peace was real.

Early in August the Chinks loaded us on trucks and drove us to the railroad, where we were put in boxcars and started south. This was the long-awaited train ride they had promised us when we started the death march way back in January of 1951. We ate canned beef and crackers on the train and in two days we were in Panmunjom. They took us to the Chinese assembly area, a big building right in the heart of town, and said they were repatriating about seventy-five G.I.'s a day.

I figured that I would be one of the last to get shipped back because of my reactionary record. Then on the afternoon of the 17th, before they read off the names of men to be released the next day, an instructor from my old company at Camp 1 called me over. He asked me what I would do if my name was called off that night. I said, nothing, I'd just act the way I always did. He wanted to know if I thought my name would be called that night. I said no, because of my record. The instructor said I might have a pleasant surprise and warned me to obey the rules and regulations while I was still under Chinese control.

That little talk sort of prepared me for what was coming. Sure enough my name was on the list. I felt

so good I couldn't explain it. That night I couldn't
sleep. I lay in my sack and thought about all the
things I had done and seen as a prisoner. I thought
over the scores I had to settle with certain men, Gallagher being on top of the list. Then I made a list of
names to give the Army, a list of reactionaries I hadn't
seen in a long time. I wanted to make damn sure that
the Chinks sent them back.

The next day we ate, rolled up our gear, and
boarded trucks. We were twelve men to a truck and
ours was the last to leave. It was a thirty or forty
minute drive to Freedom Village, which was just a
gate and some tents, but it had something we hadn't
seen in over two years. There were Americans there,
the M.P.'s and all. They had everything from generals
to privates to welcome us back. I felt light-hearted
and giddy-headed and everything else. Some old
Marine sergeant came over to the truck to call out
our names. He looked so good to me I could have
hugged him right there.

As I came down from the truck and my feet
touched the ground, I turned and made a grab for
the Chink guard to give him a good-by love tap. He
must have had experience with repatriated prisoners
because all I could see were his damn heels going
around the end of the truck. The big Marine sergeant

grabbed me and said not to worry about the Chinks. He said we would all get another crack at them pretty soon.

The Army loaded us on ambulances and started for a hospital area. I was so damn sick of the Chinese and their cruddy uniforms, I ripped my clothes off and threw them out the back of the ambulance. I was taking my shorts off when the driver told me there would be Red Cross women where we were going and that I'd better keep them on.

In the hospital we were given soap and towels and we took showers. It was my first shower in about three years. As we came out of the shower, they gave us pajamas and bathrobes and our mail from home. We were still reading the letters when they served our first American meal. I still remember the menu— roast beef, gravy, mashed potatoes, sweet peas, milk, and ice cream. They didn't make the meal too heavy because we couldn't handle rich food yet.

I asked the Army to let me hang around Freedom Village for a few days so I could meet Gallagher and a few other progressives when they arrived, but they wouldn't let me. We were put aboard helicopters and flown to Inchon, where we were issued clothing and a few hundred dollars in partial back pay. The back pay was more than we'd expected, because we all

had been automatically promoted one grade a month after our capture. I'd been a sergeant since February, 1951, without knowing it. I had my picture taken at Inchon and sent it to my mother. Three days later we boarded the U.S.S. *Marine Adder* and sailed for San Francisco.

As soon as we set sail, the Counter-Intelligence Corps started an interrogation. The C.I.C. men were all over that ship. They wanted to know everything from the day we were captured to the day the Chinese released us. It was at this time that they asked about the progressives, what they did and how they did it. They asked whether the progressives had helped or harmed the other men. Then they asked about the Chinese. Were there any friendly Chinese? What were their names? How did they help you? They asked the same questions about the Koreans. At this time most of us were in no condition to go into details. We were just too excited about being turned loose.

It took fifteen days to cross the Pacific. The C.I.C. men questioned us every day. Gallagher and some of the other big pros hadn't been released yet and I kept thinking about the look of surprise that would be on their faces when they came back and the C.I.C. got ahold of them. It didn't turn out the way I had pic-

tured because the Army took years to catch up with some of the progressives.

So far I've only named a few of the known progressives. There was only one man I wanted to see really brought to justice and that was Gallagher. I hadn't made any promises about the others and I'm leaving it up to the American government to expose these men if it sees fit. If the Army doesn't think their crimes were bad enough for prosecution, I'm not going to name them and cause them trouble. But I can say that some of the men who came back were worse than the twenty-one turncoats who stayed with the Chinese after the armistice.

We landed in San Francisco on the 5th of September and the Army took us to the hospital at the Presidio for another checkup. From there we telephoned home at the expense of the Red Cross. It sure did sound good to hear my mother's voice again. We were both so full of feeling that we couldn't talk much. The next morning I caught a plane for the East Coast. The end of my journey was Columbia, South Carolina. It's my home town and all my people were at the airport.

The Army sent me to the hospital at Fort Jackson, South Carolina, so I could be near home while I underwent treatment. I had a goiter from malnutrition

and lack of iodine. My sinus trouble was very bad and I was weak and underweight. They kept me in the hospital on and off until December when I was well enough to return to duty.

While I was on leave from the hospital, I walked into a ten-cent store in Camden, South Carolina. I saw a pretty, dark-haired girl working in there and I walked up and asked her if she was wasn't Juanita Branham who had gone to the third grade with me in the Pine Grove Grammar School near Camden. She didn't remember me but I had the right girl all right. We started going around together and we were married on December 31, 1953, just three years after the Chinks captured me.

At that time I thought I would be able to forget all about Chinks and the rats in prison camps, but it wasn't the way things turned out.

Thirteen

WHEN I took my basic training early in 1950, most people thought the next war was going to be fought with push buttons and public opinion was against rugged training for recruits. The bayonet was regarded as an obsolete weapon and not once during my fourteen weeks of basic did I so much as see one.

Just eight months later I was under fire in an old-fashioned war in Korea. You can imagine my surprise when our first action turned out to be hand-to-hand fighting and the first North Korean I saw jumped up and was fixing to run me through with his obsolete bayonet.

I didn't even know what to do with my bayonet. All I could do was step back and shoot him with my

M-1 rifle. This was a very bad tactic to use in hand-to-hand fighting because my rifle bullet went clear through the Gook. If there had been any G.I.'s behind him, that bullet could have killed them.

It was thinking back over this incident and others like it that made me decide to stay in the Army after I came back to this country. I figured I had learned some things the hard way in combat and in prison camps that could save American lives in the next war and I re-enlisted to teach them to young soldiers.

In the beginning, when I began to leave the hospital at Fort Jackson and went around to talk to G.I.'s in training on the post, I came close to getting fed up with the Army. The recruits seemed to resent the Army for pulling them into service and taking them from their civilian jobs. They thought training was a laugh and told me how they had got their non-coms and officers chewed out by writing home to their mothers, or to the Inspector General, or by crying on the chaplain's shoulder.

It's not the place of a sergeant to lecture the Army on how to do things or to tell the American people how to run their Army, but I wouldn't be honest if I didn't take this chance to tell an important thing I learned: The Army is very capable of taking care of

its men and teaching them how to survive in combat. This calls for rugged training and the public should not try to stop the Army from getting men ready in the ways it knows are best.

I'll never forget one case of civilian interference. It was back in 1950 and things were pretty rugged in Korea. A brewing company back in the States told the Army it wanted to send some free beer to the men in Korea. And don't think we wouldn't have liked to come off the front lines and sit down for a few minutes to enjoy a beer.

The Army thought the idea was okay, but a bunch of women got their heads together and had their clubs and organizations jump all over the Army. "Don't send our boys beer," they said. "Send them fruit juices instead." And the Army did.

I hope some of these women read this. Because I feel they would be glad to know that we used their cans of fruit juice for target practice. This is just one example of the way that people who don't know a thing about it stick their noses in the business of the Army.

It happens in other ways. Say a man comes into the Army and he doesn't like it. He thinks it's too rough for him and he sits down and writes his mother a long sob story. She takes the letter to her preacher

or women's clubs and they write to a Congressman. Then the politician writes to the commander of this boy's post. The letter gets passed right down the line until finally some non-com or junior officer gets reprimanded for trying to make this boy learn something that may save his life later on.

What happens when this man gets into combat? He can't sit down and write a letter saying, "Mom, they're shooting at me." The mother can't write the Congressman and he won't write the enemy and say, "Stop shooting at that boy. He's a clean-cut American boy and he doesn't like to be shot at."

When this man gets into combat he's going to wonder why he wasn't taught in basic what he should know, why they didn't show him what to expect and what to do. And when the mother gets a missing-in-action telegram and the politician looks over the casualty lists, everybody is going to stop and wonder why.

From the end of 1953 to July of 1955, I was an instructor at Camp Gordon, Georgia. I taught technique of fire, squad tactics, scouting and patrolling—all important subjects. They not only can save a man's life, but a whole squad. We couldn't make the problems very realistic because the men were always writ-

ing home and telling how close they came to being killed. They were exaggerating the point, trying to sound big to the folks back home, but the folks back home were putting pressure on the Army.

Nobody in the Army today believes in abusing or maiming young soldiers. But sometimes they are mule-headed and you can't even use profanity in front of them without getting busted. There are some soldiers who will not do what you tell them no matter how many times you say it. I have seen one boot in in the behind turn these men into the best damn soldiers you ever saw. The Army and they are better off for it, but it's against the law.

It is no longer enough to teach a young soldier how to fight in combat. He should also know how to survive and how to behave in a prison camp if he ever gets captured. The Army learned a lot from the Korean War and our men are now getting better training in everything from bayonet fighting to how to resist Communist brainwashing.

There is the matter of food. A lot of soldiers, especially young recruits, gripe about Army chow. They say they don't like it and they sneak off to the PX to stuff themselves with hot dogs and soft drinks. This is a bad habit to let them get into because I know men who were trained that way who didn't come

back from Korea because of it. A man should learn to eat what he gets.

The food in the Chinese prison camps was sorry. It was much worse than the slop a farmer feeds his hogs. But it would keep you alive if you ate it. You may have had to hold your nose but you could eat it. A lot of men wouldn't try. They said "I can't" because they didn't like the taste of the Chinese slop. And a lot of those men are still over there.

Another thing we can do in training is to discourage soldiers from running to their sergeants or lieutenants with tales about other men. Some non-coms will listen when a soldier tattles about another man and will thank him, but it is the worst mistake we can make with young soldiers. The habits they get into in training are the habits they take into combat and captivity. And the man who carried tales in the States was the same man who ratted to the Chinks in prison camps. We can stop them from learning that kind of thing here.

Any soldier captured by a Communist army can expect to undergo a period of brainwashing, which is just a new word for an old trick—to get a man to turn traitor against his country. When a soldier knows what to expect, he has a better chance of resisting the Communists. The Army must teach men the tricks

the Chinese used in Korea because other Communist armies, if they get the chance, will probably use the same system.

The first thing the Communists do is put the men through a starvation period. As a general rule it lasts six months. They will admit that the food is bad and the medical care is worse. But they will blame it on the Americans and say they are bombing medical convoys and supply trains.

Their purpose during the starvation period is to kill off the weak and wounded soldiers. It isn't true that the Communists want to convert the weakest men. They want only the men with the strongest will to live to be left because they think they can make better Communists out of them.

All through these first six months they give short lectures on Communism, nothing very heavy. They start by telling about the bad points of the American government. Then they go into the good points of Communism. The whole idea is to get the men to start doubting their own country.

By this time the Communists will have selected the men they think are really falling for their line. These men they take aside for an advanced Communist course with lectures about the theories of Marx, Engels, Lenin and Stalin. They will say all this stuff is

above the head of the average prisoner and this appeals to the men they have picked.

Then they dream up some idea and try to push it over. In Korea it was about germ warfare. It's very important to them to get the men to participate in the program by signing petitions, making voice recordings, and writing articles. They try to make the men do something, no matter how small. Then they hold that over their heads, telling them they will be punished for it when they get home. Once a man does that small favor for them, they've got him where they want him.

In the cases of some men in Korea, the Communists tried to force them to co-operate by using threats of punishment or death. These cases were very rare because as a rule they don't have to force a man; there were more than enough who willingly co-operated with them.

All the while they hammer on unemployment and racial segregation in the United States, that soldiers are the underdogs of the war, and that there are men sitting back in the United States getting rich and fat off the war.

During most of their lectures, they will bring up incidents from American history and politics. Usually the Communist instructors are much better edu-

cated on the facts than the average soldier and it is very possible for them to twist the facts around to meet their own needs.

It is right at this point where we can stop them. If our soldiers are taught American history and politics and about how the economic system works in the United States, they will be able to argue against the lies the Communists tell them. The Army can do some of this, but not all. It's mostly up to the soldier's parents and his school and church before he gets into the Army.

I remember one line the Communists were very successful with. They kept throwing up the fact that the American government had taken shiploads of potatoes and dumped them in the ocean. Their argument was that the government should have taken these potatoes and sold them to poor people at low prices. A lot of men never knew that the reason for dumping the potatoes was to save the farmers who grew them. It was very easy for the Chinese to begin converting men on this point alone.

After a while they start criticism meetings. At first you are supposed to criticize yourself. Later they insist that you criticize or inform on other men. Gradually they try to set men against one another. They tell you that a good Communist informs on every-

body. These criticism meetings can get a lot of rats started.

In Korea there were some well-educated men in my P.W. company. Some of them went with the Communists, others resisted them. The Chinks knew that the educated men were in the way of the indoctrination program, and those who wouldn't work with them were threatened into keeping their mouths shut. Education in itself didn't seem to have too much to do with whether a man turned progressive or reactionary. We had educated men and illiterates on both sides. But pride in themselves, and their country, or stubbornness in holding to their ideas, or just plain hate for the enemy kept most of the men straight that I knew.

In our camps there were some men who were ready to swing over to the Chinese even before the indoctrination program was really rolling. Back in the States and in the Army these men were brown-nosers, bullies and show-offs. All the Chinks had to do in Korea was give them a chance to show their true colors.

On November 6, 1954, at Camp Gordon, the Army awarded me the Commendation Ribbon for the way I acted in the prison camps. I would have preferred to have won my decoration on the battlefield but I

bring it up because the man who wrote the citation summed up how to resist the Communists better than I can. This is what he wrote; I admit it makes me proud:

"Sergeant Lloyd W. Pate, Infantry, United States Army, distinguished himself by meritorious service while a prisoner of war in North Korea. . . . He organized groups of fellow prisoners to disrupt attempts at Communist indoctrination and harass their instructors. Each time the groups were disbanded because of informants, Sergeant Pate formed other resistance groups.

"He also personally and openly voiced his true opinions, punished confirmed informers and in other ways obstructed the Communist indoctrination program. In spite of repeated severe punishment, he steadfastly defied all attempts at indoctrination and encouraged fellow prisoners of war to resist.

"By his courageous example and leadership, he raised the morale of fellow prisoners, stiffened their resistance and contributed in great measure to the failure of the Communist program to convert prisoners of war to communism. Sergeant Pate's outstanding devotion to duty reflects credit upon himself and the military service."

Some men in the prison camps thought that by

co-operating with the Communists they could improve their food and living conditions to a great extent, but they were wrong. The progressives in Korea sometimes got a few favors and a little better food, but nothing to make it worth while. The other prisoners could have got the same food if they'd stuck together.

I remember several times in the camps our food dropped way below average, and average was pretty bad. A large group of the prisoners got together and refused to eat the food or listen to the Communist lectures. The food immediately improved. This didn't happen just once or twice, but a number of times.

The most important thing the Army can teach its soldiers about captivity is that they are stronger than the enemy if they stick together. The Chinks knew this and they were afraid of it. That's why they tried to set us against each other and it is why they backed down when we refused to eat their slop or listen to their lies.

From experience as a P.W., I know that if soldiers stay together in every way, take care of their sick and weak, buck each other up when the going gets rough, and resist the enemy in every way, he won't be able to brainwash or convert any one of them. He'll be sick and tired of prisoners who act that way and

he'll want to get the war over sooner to get rid of them.

Not too long ago President Eisenhower issued a new code of conduct for prisoners of war. I agree with every word in it especially the part about not telling the enemy a damn thing except your name, age, rank and serial number. And one section in the code summed up how a man should feel:

"If I am captured I will continue to resist by all means available. I will make every effort to escape and aid others to escape. I will accept neither parole nor special favors from the enemy."

In the code, the President also said:

"I will never forget that I am an American fighting man, responsible for my actions, and dedicated to the principles which made my country free. I will trust in my God and in the United States of America."

We didn't know these words when we were in Korea but many of us had that thought in mind all during our time in the prison camps. I know that at any time we wouldn't have been surprised to see Patton tanks come rolling over the hills after the Chinks. This thought helped us keep going.

The soldier who allows himself to be indoctrinated not only lets down his country, but he doesn't even win any respect from the enemy. I was asked by

several Chinese what had happened to the diehard American soldier of World War II. After seeing the way P.W.'s were denying their country, the Chinks said they were ashamed to admit they had fought alongside the Americans in that war.

They had no use for the reactionaries—that's for sure. We meant trouble for them. But they never had as much contempt for us as they had for the men who worked with them.

A man who is captured should remember he is still capable of fighting back even though he is a prisoner and no longer has his weapons. No matter how small a thing may seem, if he will go ahead and do it against the enemy, it may develop into something big. He must always be on the lookout for the chance to kill or harass the enemy. When the opportunity comes, he should be able and ready to make the most of it.

If we train our recruits in this way, if we teach them about old weapons like the bayonet and how to handle all the new ones, if we give the men training soldiers more authority, if we make the discipline strict and fair, the next time we need an Army we'll have fewer men taken prisoner and these will be men we can be proud of.

Fourteen

I WAS training troops at Camp Gordon on July 1, 1955, when the Army suddenly ordered me to report to Fort Jay on Governors Island in New York City. They wanted me as a witness in a court martial. The case was the United States Army *vs.* Sergeant James C. Gallagher and the charge was murder.

In a way I had been expecting the orders ever since the Chinese let us out of their prison camps in North Korea and we told the Counter-Intelligence Corps what had gone on there. It did sort of surprise me that it took the Army almost two years to get around to Gallagher, but I felt that they had used the time to investigate the case thoroughly before they decided to draw up charges against the man.

It was no fun to leave my wife and our baby boy,

who was six months old then. I took the train to New York and then the ferry to Governors Island, where I learned that Gallagher was charged with unpremeditated murder of three G.I.'s in Camp 5, maltreatment of these men, general collaboration with the enemy, and informing on me and my squad. He could get life in prison on these charges.

My first assignment was to report to Major James J. Jenkins, the trial counsel, who is like the prosecutor in a civilian trial. He had an assistant, Lieutenant Erwin B. Drucker, and the two of them wanted to find out everything I knew about Gallagher—facts in his favor as well as things against him.

The two officers questioned me for a short time every day for about a week. The stories I had to tell them brought back things about the prison camps that I had wanted to forget and had forgotten. I just had to relive them again. I started having nightmares, waking up at all hours of the night in a cold sweat. Those were the first nightmares I had about Korea since I first came back to the States.

I told Major Jenkins that I was the only man present who could testify to the court about having seen Gallagher hang that poor G.I. on the peg and throw him out dead in the snow. And I was the only man who had been in the Chinese headquarters the day I

heard him advise the Chinks to shoot me and my squad.

When we talked about these things, I told him I never thought for a minute that Gallagher would be convicted on what I had to say. I figured it was only my word against his and in the eyes of the trial board his word would be as good as mine.

Major Jenkins told me not to worry about it. He said I should just tell the truth the way I had heard it and seen it and we would leave it up to the trial board to decide whether the man was guilty or not and whether they could believe my testimony. He told me that my evidence would help the board see the pattern in which the man worked and that my testimony would be of value.

There was only one thing I enjoyed about the whole time on Governors Island and that was seeing some of the guys from my old squad there. They had also been called as witnesses against Gallagher. It was great to know that they had made it back alive. Some of the men I hadn't seen since the Chinks took me away after our court-martial and sent me to the jail at Camp 2 in September of 1952.

At the trial we had Vernon Clark, Donnell Adams, Alfred McMillan, Willie Dorrill, and Preston Hibbard, all from the reactionary squad. Cletys Nordin,

my buddy from combat who had been our spy in Chinese headquarters, was also there. We talked a lot about life in Korea and what we had done since then. All of us had got married and we all had stayed in the Army except Nordin, who was working for Skelly Oil in Oklahoma, and Dorrill, who had started a hog farm in Alabama.

Since Nordin and Dorrill were civilians, they were stationed in quarters for the officers on Governors Island. The rest of us were put in with the enlisted men and that turned out to be rough. By some accident the Army had put us in with the same company Gallagher had served with before he had been indicted and put in the stockade. It turned out that after he came back, he re-enlisted in the Army and tried to be a good soldier. He was well liked by all the officers and enlisted men in the company.

There was quite a bit of resentment against us among the men in Gallagher's company. They even spread rumors that we were trying to frame him. They never said it to our faces, but we could overhear them talking about it. I heard the men say that it was all a frame-up deal, that we had a personal grudge against Gallagher, and that we were trying to take it out on him by testifying against him.

Later on, during the trial and after it was over, a

lot of these same men came up to us and apologized for the things they had said. Some of them were in the courtroom listening to the evidence and they told the other men about it. They admitted that when they had talked about a frame-up, they hadn't known anything about the case and what went on in Korea.

I saw Gallagher only once before the trial started. He was coming out of the defense counsel's office and I was going in. He looked very neat in his summer uniform with the sergeant's stripes on his sleeves and I must admit he looked like a soldier, not the bully I knew in Korea. All except his eyes—he had the look of a little whipped puppy in them.

I said, "Hi, Gallagher, how you doing?"

"Okay, Pate," he said. "How about you?"

"Aw, so so," I said and walked away. There didn't seem to be any point in saying anything else. He knew why I was there and I knew what I had to do and that was it.

At that point I began to feel sorry for Gallagher for the first time. I'd been a prisoner myself and I hated to see any man confined to jail. Even though I hated this man for what he had done, I still couldn't help but feel sorry for him. Right then, if I hadn't made that promise to the dead kid in Korea, I would have walked out and gone home and not testified.

The only reason I stayed to testify at the trial was that I felt sure if there were any doubt in the minds of the trial board, this man would not be found guilty. I knew if they were not satisfied with the testimony, they would turn him loose. And I was sure he would receive a much fairer trial than my squad got from the Chinese on August 4, 1952, when my defense counsel didn't say a word.

Gallagher's trial opened on the first day of August. In the Army courts witnesses are kept in a special witness room and I wasn't present except when I was on the stand. I didn't learn a hell of a lot about the trial because witnesses are forbidden to discuss testimony among themselves.

At the worst part of the trial I wasn't in the courtroom. This was when Donnell Adams and five other men—some from my squad and some other prisoners —testified how Gallagher had got mad at the stink from two kids who were sick from dysentery and too weak to clean themselves up and how he had thrown them out of the hut to die in the snow. This happened before I came to Camp 5 and I didn't have any firsthand knowledge of it.

The next day I learned from the newspapers that the two G.I.'s had been Corporal John W. Jones, from Detroit, and Corporal Donald T. Baxter, from

Waukon, Iowa. They were both young kids. The papers said that Jones' mother and his sister had come from Detroit to attend the trial and find out how the boy had died. The testimony must have been awful for them to hear.

Nearly every day of the trial I came face to face with Gallagher. We talked to each other and he never showed any resentment against me. I had told him a long time before what I was going to do to bring him to justice and I gave him years to get ready for it. I didn't sneak up on him.

On the eighth day of the trial they called me to the stand. I just gave my testimony about seeing Gallagher hang that soldier on the peg in the wall. Then I told the court-martial about how I had overheard him tell the Chinks they could put over their indoctrination program by shooting me and my squad. I testified that he had given the Chinese his wholehearted support, collaborated with them, backed up everything they had to say, and circulated a petition for them.

The hardest thing about the trial was to have to get up in front of Gallagher's mother and his sisters and tell them what I had seen and what kind of a guy he was. They seemed to be nice people. I have had to do many hard things in my life but that was

the hardest. It was obvious to me that they adored this boy and it was tough to paint a bad picture of him when they had such a different idea.

Then the defense counsel went to work on me. In his cross-examination he hammered hard at my testimony and wanted to know if I had a grudge against Gallagher. I said I didn't and that the man had never done me any harm. All I held against him was hanging that man on the wall and collaborating with the enemy. I said I did not hold it against him for trying to have me shot because I felt all along that the Chinese would not shoot me and I didn't worry too much about it.

When Gallagher took the stand he called me a liar. He told a different story about the hanging. He said the dead boy's name was Dunn and he was weak from pneumonia and very lazy. An English doctor in the camp said Dunn needed exercise but he wouldn't walk around and Gallagher got tired holding him up. So Gallagher rigged up a scarf under the boy's shoulders and hung the scarf on the peg in the wall so the boy could get exercise by walking in the air. That was his explanation for what I had seen.

I was called back on the stand and asked to draw a diagram of the building in which I had seen the hanging. They also called on me to testify about Gal-

lagher's calling me a liar and I went through the story again. Then they asked me a few more questions and excused me as a witness.

Just as I had expected, the trial board didn't find Gallagher guilty of murdering that boy. But they did convict him of maltreatment for hanging the kid on the peg. The board also didn't find him guilty of trying to get my squad shot, just of informing on us to the Chinks. Six guys had testified about the deaths of Jones and Baxter and he was convicted of killing them by throwing them out in the snow. He was also found guilty of collaborating with the enemy.

I didn't know all this at the time, because as soon as I was excused as a witness I caught the first train back to Augusta, where my wife and baby were. I didn't want to stay for the verdict and didn't make any effort to find out about it—never picked up a newspaper, never turned on the radio. The reason was that I was fed up with the trial and the memories it brought back. When I got home my nerves were shot to hell. My feelings about ratting were so strong that I felt bad for having testified, even against a rat.

A few days after I got back, I was in a grocery store in Augusta. The story about the Gallagher trial had been in all the newspapers and the salesgirl asked me how I'd enjoyed my trip up North. I said I

didn't. There was a man in the store who probably had seen my picture in the papers. He said, "I see where Gallagher got life."

"Yeah," I said and just walked out. Then I began to think. Life—the worst sentence a man could get. I thought about the thirty-one months and nineteen days I had been a prisoner, and about Gallagher being only twenty-four and having a long way to go before his life term would be over.

I felt lousy because an ex-P.W. always feels for a prisoner. And in a way I felt good. I just thought to myself that I fulfilled my promise to that dead kid.

I hope the kid, whoever he is, is resting easier over there. Maybe now he's happy.

Te Deum

Thanks be to God for His love
and mercy,

Thanks be to God for His
boundless grace,

Thanks be to God for the hearts
that love us,

Thanks be to God for each
friendly face.

Thanks be to God for strength
in suffering,

Thanks be to God for joys
we've known,

Thanks be to God for the hope
He gives us

Of rest eternal beside His
Throne.

Joe Kotcka

525A

DESIGN COPR. 1955 DEVOTIONAL PUBLISHING CO. LITHO IN U.S.A.